HOT
COUNTRY
Women

MIKE KOSSER

AVON BOOKS ◆ NEW YORK

HOT COUNTRY WOMEN is an original publication of Avon Books. This work has never before appeared in book form.

AVON BOOKS
A division of
The Hearst Corporation
1350 Avenue of the Americas
New York, New York 10019

Copyright © 1994 by Mike Kosser
Cover and interior photographs by Alan L. Mayor
Published by arrangement with the author
Library of Congress Catalog Card Number: 94-94068
ISBN: 0-380-77585-9

First Avon Books Printing: August 1994

AVON TRADEMARK REG. U.S. PAT. OFF. AND IN OTHER COUNTRIES, MARCA REGISTRADA, HECHO EN U.S.A.

Printed in the U.S.A.

OPM   10   9   8   7   6   5   4   3   2   1

Acknowledgments

Back in 1992 I started on the first book of this series, called *Hot Country*, which focused on the premier male stars of country music. The success of that book was so gratifying that a sequel about the women seemed like a great idea.

Like *Hot Country*, this book was possible only because of the unselfish help I received from Martha Sharp, Pat Rolfe, Susan Longacre, Bobby Braddock, Frank Dycus, Jim Foglesong, John Vezner, Ed Morris, Dan Gordon, Woody Bowles, Michelle Wright, Celinda Pink, Alan Mayor, Buzz Ledford, and Vernell Hackett.

I would also like to give special thanks to Ronnie Pugh and the Country Music Foundation and its unparalleled archives of country music documents and information.

Finally, thanks to my wife Gina, and our children, Alan and Rebecca, for keeping me smiling on days when the computer wouldn't boot properly.

COUNTRY'S BEST—AND BEAUTIFUL

REBA MCENTIRE

Once she was a rodeo queen from Oklahoma. Now she's #1 on the charts—with two double platinum albums at the same time.

DOLLY PARTON

She not only made it as a superstar singer, but as an actress, writer, publisher, and top-notch businesswoman—and she's never forgotten where she came from or how hard life can be.

TRISHA YEARWOOD

The daughter of a Georgia schoolteacher, she went from session singer to star—with a little help from Garth Brooks along the way.

PATTY LOVELESS

Born in Kentucky coal country, she went through as much hard luck as any heartbreaker song—and it almost ended her career.

MARY CHAPIN CARPENTER

A solid platinum country star who was born with a silver spoon, she's an Ivy Leaguer who picked up a guitar and turned herself into a Hot Country Woman.

PLUS: TANYA TUCKER, LORRIE MORGAN, SUZY BOGGUSS, PAM TILLIS, KATHY MATTEA . . . AND THE NEWEST UP-AND-COMING STARS IN COUNTRY MUSIC.

Other Avon Books By
Mike Kosser

HOT COUNTRY

Contents

1

Country Women Come of Age

THE COUNTRY WOMEN HAVE ARRIVED. AFTER A HALF century of domination by male performers, country music has finally made room for a group of female singers so powerful and appealing that they are giving the boys a run for their money, over the airwaves and off the record racks.

Only two years ago I was talking to a record executive at a major label in Nashville. He was thrilled with his roster of new young male artists. "This one is going gold next week. . . . That one has the best new album I've ever heard, he's gonna be a big star," and so on.

"What about the girls?" I asked.

"Don't ask," was his answer. He wrinkled up his nose as if I'd asked him how they were doing with their singing animal acts. "We've got two girls on the label and we can't get anything happening with them and we're *not* looking for girl acts."

A year later I was having lunch with him in one of those restaurants near Nashville's Music Row that does a big expense account business. By this time the girls in country music were no secret, and his tone had changed.

"Oh yeah. We've got this new girl who will knock your cap in the creek," he said, or something like that. "And we've got this girl that we're signing next week and, Kosser, you gotta hear her!''

The boys may still be outselling the girls by five to one, but the women have made progress that nobody on Music Row would have suspected more than a decade back, when the main, hot-selling female star was Dolly Parton. And she was selling mostly on the basis of her pop audience, so you might say that in those days there were *no* hot-selling female country stars.

As this book is being written, there are a solid dozen female acts that are making it big in country music, with more on the way. These women have not only helped to revolutionize the stature of women in country music, they also have helped to change the attitudes of those who listen to country music.

Country music, more than any other American popular music, looks at what is happening across America, adds some rhyme, melody, and rhythm, and passes it back to us in a form that hits us in the heart. The truth is that throughout the history of country music, female singers sang songs written by men voicing men's ideas of what women were supposed to feel. Yet most relationships between men and women are punctuated by quarrels based on the inability of men to understand the way women feel and vice versa. The idea that male songwriters should possess an insight denied most other men is ridiculous. Perhaps the reason there were so few big-selling country women was the limits put on their material by the men who wrote it.

No matter. Today some of the women sing their own material, and there is a whole new breed of female songwriters out there writing about what women *really* feel.

In this book I'll talk about the top female singers, how they got where they are, their lives, their loves, and what they feel about many things.

For the past two decades country music has been threatening to become *the* music of middle America: the music

The Women of Country Music TV show in 1992 features (l to r) Emmylou Harris, Kathy Mattea, Trisha Yearwood, Pam Tillis, Patty Loveless, Suzy Bogguss, and Mary Chapin Carpenter.

that crosses age barriers, class barriers, and education barriers more than any music since before the dawn of rock and roll. And now that country music is there, the women in country music are having a strong influence on millions of women across America.

Turn the pages of this book. Take a look at the pictures and read the stories of today's women in country music. Some of them are stars and superstars. Some of them are mighty forces behind the scenes. Some of them are women on the way up, and some of them are still struggling with a mighty spirit against daunting odds.

But all of them have strong wills and the rugged determination to fight the good fight that success in the music business requires. It is impossible to convey completely just how tough it is to make it on Music Row. I hope, in the pages of this book, to give the readers an idea of just what kind of heart it takes to be one of the hottest women in country music today.

2

A Short Oral History

WOMEN HAVE BEEN A PART OF THE COUNTRY RE-cording scene since way back in the 1920s, according to Ronnie Pugh of the Country Music Foundation. The Country Music Foundation is the organization responsible for the Country Music Hall of Fame and for priceless archives of American country music.

I decided to let Ronnie give me a brief history of the girls in country music:

"You go all the way back to a Samantha Bumgarner in the twenties who recorded on the Okeh label," he said, pointing out that she is often considered the first female country vocalist to record. "Much better known than her would be Moonshine Kate, who was Rosa Lee Carson, the daughter of Fiddlin' John Carson. She recorded with her father very very early.

"You had some cowgirls as early as the late twenties. Billy Maxwell is the one who comes to my mind; . . . of course, two thirds of the famous Carter Family were women, and they were certainly more important than anything A. P. [Carter] did on the record. He was a kind of songfinder, but you had Sarah and Maybelle who both vocally and instrumentally were central to that famous group.

"Historically the first woman to have a million seller [in country music] was Patsy Montana, another cowgirl, and it was 'I Wanna Be a Cowboy's Sweetheart' in 1935. You didn't have RIAA then, [the organization that, among other things, authenticates the sales of records today] so you're never going to find certification on those sales, and some people question it, but it's been passed around orally; it's part of country music folklore now, that Patsy did it. And she's still performing . . . Cousin Emmy is a favorite of the folk enthusiasts—now deceased, of course . . . she was around Atlanta a lot of the time . . . she was a Kentucky native. You had Rose Maddox with her brothers, they were usually called the Maddox Brothers and Rose, performing out in California. They were . . . transplanted Okies. They were based out there from the time they were just kids in the late thirties, and Rose also still performs today. Women have *long* careers. Most of her brothers have passed away, but Rose is [still active]. She even did duets with Buck Owens in the sixties, you might remember, but she started as a kid in the thirties.

"Molly O'Day," Pugh continued, "was a great favorite of Uncle Art Satherley, the Columbia Records boss for so many years. She was also a native of Kentucky like Cousin Emmy, and she was based around Knoxville when she recorded for Columbia right after the war in 1946. She was the first to record a Hank Williams song. I think it was 'Six More Miles to the Graveyard.' Uncle Art loved Molly's singing and it *was* good. She recorded for about four years, and then went full time into gospel work and quit recording until Old Homestead [Records] found her in her later years. She passed away in the late eighties.

"During the war you had acts like the Girls of the Golden West, a cowgirl duet. They actually predate the war. [They were] based around Cincinnati [and] recorded for Bluebird. You had Jennie Lou Carson, who was based in Chicago . . . she was the sister-in-law of Red Foley . . . she's known more as a writer than a singer although she made some pretty good records. Fred Rose [great song-writer publisher and Hank Williams's mentor] was *deeply* attached to Jennie Lou Carson. Maybe [it was] a little more than a friendship, but some of Fred's songwriting ability rubbed off on Jennie Lou.

"And then, Cindy Walker, a native Texan, first came to the fore in the war years out in California—she had moved out there—and she successfully pitched some songs to O. W. Mayo, the manager of Bob Wills. Bob had moved from Tulsa to the West Coast by then. Bob recorded several of her songs and, of course, her writing since then, and she's *still* going, has just been legendary: 'In the Misty Moonlight,' 'Distant Drums,' a lot of Jim Reeves hits, Hank Snow hits, and Ernest Tubb hits.

"There were some all-girl groups at Renfro Valley. I'm thinking of the Coon Creek Girls mostly; made some records, they weren't big hits, but Lily Mae Ledford was in that group, and so they were pretty important. . . ."

Now, the sense you get from Ronnie Pugh's overview is that in the earlier country music years, female singers were not exactly household names to the American public. While men like Jimmie Rodgers, Ernest Tubb, Hank Snow, Eddy Arnold, Hank Williams, and others were selling tons of records and having long-performing careers, in general the girl singer was somebody the star of the show introduced, usually as "pretty little somebody-or-other," to do a couple of songs and then yield the stage back to the big guy. To be honest, in America in those days many people regarded female performers as women who in some way compromised their virtue simply by making a career in singing, although if the truth be known, it was the guys who did most of the fooling around on the road.

"You have to take note of what Patsy Montana and Molly O'Day did, and they had their following," says Ronnie, "but they didn't have the sustained following of Kitty Wells."

Back in the early fifties, Fred Rose, the king of Nashville music publishers, dubbed Kitty Wells the queen of country music, and the title stuck. By today's standards, Kitty was a most unlikely queen of country music, but in those days Kitty was perfect. Born Muriel Deason in Nashville, August

30, 1919, she married country singer Johnny Wright at the
age of eighteen and was the girl singer with the popular
country act Johnny and Jack in several cities around the
South, including Knoxville, Greensboro, and Shreveport,
where they became regulars on the famous "Louisiana
Hayride" radio show. It was Lowell Blanchard in Knoxville who said that "Muriel Deason" was not going to cut
it as a stage name.

" 'Let's give her something simpler,' " Blanchard said
(according to Pugh), " 'something the country fans might
relate to,' and so they picked Kitty Wells, which was the
name of the old folk song."

In 1952 they returned to Nashville and joined the Grand
Ole Opry, and soon after that Kitty recorded "It Wasn't
God Who Made Honky Tonk Angels," which initially sold
eight hundred thousand copies and eventually went on to
sell a million. Over the next decade she had twenty-three
number one records and became country music's first great
female recording star.

Kitty was perfect as the pioneer girl country star because
of what she was. Kitty had gotten performing out of her
system fairly early in her life and had a strong ambition to
be a mother and homemaker, which she was. She was a
singer because she was part of her husband's stage act, but
when "Honky Tonk Angels" broke through, she became a
necessary part of the act. When she sang onstage, women
did not look sideways at their husbands to see if they were
fantasizing about Kitty. Women trusted Kitty. She sang
songs about them, for them. It may be hard for a young
person to listen to a Kitty Wells record today and understand why she was so popular, but to the small town and
country women of the fifties, Kitty came across as good,
kind, decent, honest.

She was. And she is today.

In the days of Kitty Wells, and before, many women
made it into the business as part of husband-wife acts.
"James and Martha Carson," recalls Pugh, "Radio Dot and
Smoky Swann; Lulu Belle and Scotty; Texas Ruby and

Kitty Wells

Curly Fox. Kitty came out of that matrix and never really left it. She was closely managed and guarded by her husband Johnny Wright from the beginning. In fact, Johnny for years had to insist that she keep singing. She would have much rather not. She was . . . a shy, retiring person.

"She'd sung on some Johnny and Jack records . . . and she had a short career with RCA in '49 and '50, mostly gospel or heart songs, and they didn't go anywhere, so Wright, according to everything I've seen, had to do some pretty good salesmanship on Paul Cohen [head of Decca Records in Nashville during the 1950s] to get her a Decca contract."

Kitty was raising her children at the time and wanted to be a full-time mother, so Johnny must have had to sell her on the idea of a big-time country recording career. This was a time when most women did not think of any kind of career beyond the household. One of the great appeals of Kitty Wells was that women sensed from the sincere quality of her voice that she was what they were, a mother and a wife.

"When she did that first Decca session," said Pugh, "she was fortunate enough to cut an answer song to the current Hank Thompson hit. The Hank Thompson song was 'The Wild Side of Life' and her answer was 'It Wasn't God Who Made Honky Tonk Angels,' which was basically a Jay Miller composition . . . the Louisiana writer . . . and she wasn't all that crazy about the song cause [she said] well this is a worn out tune, I mean the Carters did this twenty years ago and now Hank's got a hit with it, it's 'The Great Speckled Bird' and 'I'm Thinkin' Tonight of My Blue Eyes,' which she wasn't all that crazy about. But the record just really took off."

Kitty Wells was the most unlikely recording star in the history of country music. There was nothing, absolutely nothing, theatrical or spectacular about her. Typical was the summer afternoon when her bus pulled up to a grocery in a tiny Minnesota town and out jumped the members of a Nashville country band in their western-style shirts and boots. They walked into the store, bought their cold drinks and snacks, then hopped back on the bus and continued on their way to their next performing location. A normal moment in the life of a country music road band.

Except that an hour down the road they realized that

Kitty wasn't on the bus. They had to go back and get her, she was the star of the show, and when they finally returned to the grocery, two hours after they had left, there was Kitty, sitting in front of the store in her pretty dress, patiently waiting for her band to come back and get her.

In those days the country charts were still, as songwriter great Bobby Braddock once put it, "Twenty-nine guys and Kitty Wells." "It wasn't long after Kitty hit, though," says Pugh, "that Capital signed Jean Shepard, who had sort of been discovered on the West Coast by Hank Thompson, and from 'A Dear John Letter' forward she had a lot of good records. Bill Wood's band out of Bakersfield backed her on most of those early Capitol sessions.

"[So Jean was] kind of a followup to Kitty, but there weren't many others. Not at the time."

Ah, but there was a great one on the way.

"Patsy Cline," Pugh recalled, "made her first records in 1955, but she only had one hit in the fifties and that was 'Walkin' after Midnight' in '57 . . . The [Arthur] Godfrey Show had a lot to do really with that taking off like it did because she was on it several times, a repeat winner, pluggin' that same song, and she didn't have any more hits until the early sixties."

So there were almost no major female country recording stars in the forties and very few in the fifties. It wasn't until Patsy Cline started having hits in the early sixties that the major record labels really began to believe that the girls could make money for them.

Patsy Cline's real name was Virginia Patterson Hensley. She was born in Winchester, Virginia, in 1932. Early in her teens she quit school and started working in a drug store, but mostly she wanted to sing. She was aggressive enough to talk her way onto local shows, opening for big name acts when they came through town. Eventually she impressed music business veteran Wally Fowler of the Oak Ridge Quartet, which was the gospel predecessor of the Oak Ridge Boys. Fowler told Virginia's mother that she ought to let her come to Nashville, so at the age of fifteen she did, along with her mother, sisters, and a few close friends of the family.

The king of country music, Roy Acuff, heard her and urged her to stay in town, but at that time the contingent had no money or prospects, so she went back home to her job at the drugstore and her local singing routine.

Over the next half dozen years there were some professional fits and starts, a failed marriage, and finally her 1957 appearance on Arthur Godfrey's *Talent Scouts* television show, where she sang "Walkin' after Midnight" and won first prize. Decca Records released her version as a single, which became a monster hit both in country and in pop.

But there were no major hit followups for a long time. She married Charlie Dick and tried to be Mrs. Mom, but she was still hooked on her singing career. In 1960 she joined the Grand Ole Opry, and after that she had a string of hits that made her the most successful female artist in the history of country music. "I Fall to Pieces," "Crazy," and "She's Got You," were essentially torch songs about a woman broken-hearted over a failed love affair, not unlike the kinds of songs male country artists of the day sang. All were written by male songwriters, but the stories and emotions were so universal that women took the songs to heart and bought her records by the millions.

When Patsy died in an airplane crash in 1963, it left a huge hole in country music. Since then, many record executives have searched for another Patsy Cline. As of yet, they have failed to find one. A story from the late country star Dotty West provides a window on the bigger-than-life personality of Patsy Cline.

"After the show [a benefit for the family of Jack Call, a midwestern disc jockey who had died in a car crash] I asked Patsy to ride back to Nashville with me. It was really bad and stormy, and I didn't want her to take that plane. She said she would [ride back with me] and even packed her bags.

"Then she changed her mind on the elevator. I said, 'Well, I'm gonna be worried about you in that little plane.'

And she said, 'Don't worry about me. If it's my time, Hoss, I'm goin'.' And that's the last thing she said before the elevator doors closed.'' She was thirty years old when she died.

In spite of Patsy Cline, the sixties were not good years for the women in country music. There were hundreds of number one country records during the decade. According to music journalist Robert Hilburn, only fourteen of those were recorded by female country artists.

During Patsy's heyday, one of the great songwriters was Harlan Howard, who with Hank Cochran cowrote "I Fall To Pieces." His wife Jan Howard, sang on many of Harlan's demos, and eventually she had her own successful recording career, with hits like "Rock Me Back To Little Rock" and a number of duets with Bill Anderson.

In the latter part of the sixties, Loretta Lynn exploded onto the country scene, and she provided a new dimension for female country singers in that she wrote much of her own material.

"She was just a housewife," said Ronnie Pugh, "who'd been singing in some clubs in the state of Washington, and was pushed by her husband, Doo, but [unlike Kitty Wells's husband, Johnny Wright] he certainly was not in the act; he just knew she could sing and wanted her to have confidence in herself. And she had a hit on of all things a regional label up there [in Washington], Zero Records, and the song was 'Honky Tonk Girl,' in 1960. She plugged the record and toured to promote it and got in with the Wilburn Brothers, Teddy and Doyle, here in Nashville, who got her past some pretty significant hurdles. Teddy clearly was the Fred Rose to her songwriting too."

It's fair to stop here to explain what Pugh meant by that last statement. Record company publicity often attempts to make recording artists appear bigger than life, and usually the media, both print and radio, are glad to go along with the images crafted by publicists. And so Hank Williams is generally depicted as a sensational, super-talented singer-songwriter.

While there is no challenging the fact that Hank dominated country music in a way that no artist has before or
since, the probable truth is that most of the songs credited
to Hank alone were probably smoothed over considerably
by Fred Rose, the songwriting great who was Hank's mentor and publisher. Rose, who wrote classics such as "Blue
Eyes Crying In The Rain," was himself more interested in
building a money-making legend than in advancing his own
songwriting reputation, so he was glad to remain behind
the scenes in order to build Hank's reputation as a country
music genius.

In the early 1960s the Wilburn Brothers were a powerful
force in country music. The Decca Records recording artists
had a nationally syndicated weekly country music show and
a successful publishing company.

"He [Teddy Wilburn] helped a lot of her original efforts. . . . The hits really started coming in the middle sixties: 'Woman of the World,' 'Your Squaw Is on the
Warpath,' 'Don't Come Home A-Drinkin',' and 'You Ain't
Woman Enough to Take My Man.' Teddy helped on some
of them, yes, oh yes, without taking, here again, official
credit."

This is not a put-down of either Hank or Loretta. In
country music today better than 80 percent of all country
hits are cowritten. There is no shame in the fact that Hank
and Loretta may have had help in writing many of their
hits, and in both their cases, their writing associates obviously decided to regard their contributions as mere editing
rather than creative contribution.

Note that all the major female country stars up to this
time—Kitty Wells, Patsy Cline, Loretta Lynn—all de-
pended upon men for the creative decisions that made their
careers successful. But Loretta's songwriting skills gave her
records a different viewpoint from the women who de-
pended solely upon men to write their songs for them.
Songs like "You Ain't Woman Enough to Take My Man,"
"Fist City," and "Your Squaw Is on the Warpath" de-

Loretta Lynn gets a hug from Johnny Rodriguez.

picted a woman who would fight for what she wanted rather than carrying a torch and hoping for the best.

It is too easy to assume that the songs an artist sings are windows into her soul. The record industry is extremely competitive, and the songs an artist records are more likely to reflect her and her producer's beliefs concerning what the public wants to hear and buy, rather than the artist's deepest convictions.

So don't assume that just because Tammy Wynette co-wrote and had her biggest hit with "Stand By Your Man" she was willing to follow her man into the darkest recesses of hell just because he was her man.

She was dubbed country music's First Lady of Song, and the title fit her well. Of the fourteen number one hits by female artists in the sixties, Tammy Wynette had eight of them.

Although her stage image was one of professional dignity, her recording image endeared her to the blue collar harried housewife. When they heard the catch in her voice (one songwriter said she sang like she had strep throat), when she sang about the pains and sadness of everyday women, they could picture her with a squalling baby on one arm, sweating and carrying dirty dishes to a sinkful of hot water on a humid summer day as she contemplated an afternoon of laundry.

Virginia Wynette Pugh was born in Red Bay, Alabama, May 5, 1942. "She came up here from Birmingham having been a beautician and through a divorce or two," recalled Ronnie Pugh, "and had been on the Country Boy Eddie Burns TV show there, so she had a little bit of background . . . I think she was between husbands . . . she had had the two daughters by Eupel Byrd and they were not very old at the time. Tammy herself was only in her early twenties. It was, as we all know, Billy Sherrill who said, 'Hmmm, she might have something here.' Cause she did, just literally, pitch her talents to Music Row, and Billy . . . took a chance with her . . . Sherrill became not only her producer but a major songwriting source as Tammy started hitting."

It was not only her voice that was distinctive. It was also the strong persona that Sherrill, as a producer, carved for her on the basis of the songs he chose for her, songs like "I Don't Wanna Play House," "D-I-V-O-R-C-E," "Your Good Girl Is Gonna Go Bad."

Tammy Wynette in 1974.

"Loretta, of course, also sang from the woman's point of view of broken love and cheating men and men running around and expecting the woman to forgive their man's iniquities—Loretta did that, Tammy did that. Tammy was more of an I'm gonna stand by him type, although she could certainly explore divorce and heartbreak and separation,'' says Pugh.

We have to remember that Loretta wrote quite a few more of her own hits than Tammy did, although Tammy did cowrite her biggest hit record, "Stand By Your Man," with Sherrill. Billy Sherrill was a strong-willed producer, which means that when he found a song he thought was a hit he worked hard to persuade an artist to record it.

His judgment of Tammy's material was usually sound. Tammy had a solid fifteen years at the very top of her profession. Her personal life during that time, especially involving her roller-coaster marriage to George Jones and her marriages before and after George, somehow reinforced rather than conflicted with her image as Everywoman.

Last year, just when it seemed that Tammy had moved on to that generation of country star more likely to be seen in the theaters at Branson, Missouri, than at the top of the charts, Tammy found herself soloing on a pop smash titled "Justified and Ancient" by the major British group, KLF.

From the mid-sixties through the mid-seventies no female country artist had the success of Tammy Wynette. Many male music business executives over the years have complained that the trouble with female country artists is that too many of them sound alike. But nobody has ever said that Tammy sounds like anybody else or that anybody else sounds like Tammy.

The modern era of female country artists began with Dolly Parton. Between the going of Hank Williams and the coming of Randy Travis, Dolly was the most important personality to hit the country music stage.

She came to Nashville with her uncle, Bill Owens, from Sevier County, in the mountains of eastern Tennesse, where she had been born and raised. She was, to say the least, focused on her career and determined to go after it. Early on she talked her way into an appearance on the Grand Ole Opry. She impressed Buddy Killen of the powerhouse Tree Publishing Company enough that he got her a deal on Mercury Records where, at the age of sixteen, she had her first release on a major record label titled "It's Sure Gonna

Hurt.'' The record didn't do anything, but the experience was educational. No experience has ever been wasted on Dolly.

She has her own chapter in this book, so I won't say much more about her here except that in the beginning, like all the women before her, she required the efforts and guidance of men to get her where she wanted to go. At the time she was trying to make it, men held virtually all the positions of power in country music.

But Dolly went on to hack out some new trails through the country music jungle. Once she became a country star, largely through the good offices of Porter Wagoner, her boss and duet partner, she assumed a bigger and bigger role in directing her career into areas where previous country acts, female *or* male, had seldom trod—first to the top of the pop charts, then to starring roles in successful major motion pictures, then to multiple business enterprises, and finally back to her country roots, where her fans have gladly forgiven her for wandering.

When Dolly hit it big on the pop charts with ''Here You Come Again,'' many country fans felt that she had deserted them, and she had. But in the long run her trip away from country was a good thing for country music because Dolly herself was so undeniably country that she was an eye-opener for the provincial New York and L. A. music industry veterans who believed that nothing very good could come out of the Nashville music scene.

The seventies was Dolly's country decade, but during that time quite a few women made it big in country music along with her, notably Barbara Mandrell, Crystal Gayle, Emmylou Harris, Olivia Newton-John, Linda Ronstadt, Donna Fargo, and Tanya Tucker. All of these acts went gold or platinum somewhere in their careers, and all of them still perform, but only Tanya and Dolly continue to turn out the hit records.

Country music has come a long way since the days of twenty-nine guys and Kitty Wells. In Nashville, women have not only become extraordinarily successful as artists,

Tammy Wynette with Randy Travis.

they have also succeeded in positions where women were almost never seen twenty years ago. They head music publishing companies and pitch songs, they run Artist and Repertoire (A & R) departments at record companies, where they help discover tomorrow's new stars, and they are powerful figures in management, publicity, promotion, performing rights, and almost everything else.

What is perhaps most important for country songstresses is that a host of female songwriters has emerged to bring the woman's viewpoint to the country song. It is almost laughable to think back to a time when macho songwriters took time out from their honky-tonk ballads to try and write a sensitive "girl song" because "Billy still hasn't found all the songs for Tammy."

Those male songwriters probably wrote their best material for women when they came across an idea or a feeling that was universal. When they tried to write one that Sherrill's prototype, thirty-year-old housewives, would love, the results were often not as thrilling.

In two areas, women have not come as far as they should have. First, only one major record label in Nashville is headed by a woman, and second, although many female artists coproduce their own albums, only one woman has gained a reputation as a producer of country acts, and she has left the Nashville scene, at least for now.

But otherwise, there is no doubt that women are hotter in country music than ever before. In the following pages you will read about the hottest female stars, the up and comers, and the women behind the scenes who have added so much to country music over the past decade. In some ways women have more power in country music than in any other commercial music genre. Their struggles to achieve this power have been long and difficult, and they still have a long way to go.

If you look up and down the artist rosters at the major labels, you will see that the future of women in country music is as brilliant as a country sunrise.

3

Celinda Pink

NASHVILLE IS A TYPICAL SOUTHERN RIVER TOWN THAT was kissed by fate in the form of a radio program that somehow survived when a lot of similar radio programs were buried by disc jockeys and television. The Grand Ole Opry is now the centerpiece of a business worth many millions of dollars each year to Gaylord Entertainment.

The Ryman Auditorium was, many journalists seem to think, the first home of the Grand Ole Opry. In fact, there were a number of previous homes of the Opry, including several radio studios and the War Memorial Auditorium, a stylish old edifice that is still used for highbrow events in downtown Nashville. But the Ryman became the most famous location, and because the Ryman was located just off Broadway in downtown Nashville, Broadway took on the feel of a honky-tonk street. Tootsie's, the Demon's Den, Linebaugh's, and Ernest Tubb's Record Shop all became prime destinations for tourists and music hopefuls, and even though the Opry has moved out to the suburbs, Lower Broad, as it is called, still has more than its share of neon and beer signs.

Lower Broadway hasn't quite decided what it wants to be, but it's definitely changing. The upscale yuppie shops and franchise restaurants compete with the adult bookstores for the future of the area, and in the meantime the honky-tonks remain, along with the pawnshops, guitar shops, and furniture stores. They're building a big arena there, and the Country Music Hall of Fame is moving there, too. So is the company that owns the Grand Ole Opry. Because Nashville is a good ol' southern river town, Lower Broad ends at the winding Cumberland River; the homeless people sleep under the bridges that span the river, while struggling singers and songwriters arrive on Greyhound buses and cash their money orders from home at special places down on Lower Broad.

Occasionally, one of these struggling singers gets a gig for twenty-five or fifty bucks a night singing in a Lower Broad honky-tonk. The work is hard and sweaty and the chances of being "discovered" are slim. Record industry people are one part sentimental and ninety-nine parts business. You can be the most exciting honky-tonk singer in the world, but if they don't think they can cut hit records on you, they will pass you by in a heartbeat.

And that's why Celinda Pink is such a great story. Celinda is a highly educated lady. She graduated from Lower Broad University, which is the toughest school in country music. She looks like a Lower Broad graduate, and she sounds like a Lower Broad graduate. She sings as if she gargles with glass shards, as if she's been beaten up by a hundred misogynistic rednecks. For years she was the lady for whom the record executives drove downtown to see and hear. But nobody dared take a chance on her until Buzz Ledford at Step One Records heard her and brought her to the head of the label, music veteran Ray Pennington.

After all that time as the queen of Lower Broad, Celinda Pink finally had herself a real record deal.

Celinda Pink was born Celinda Cosby in Tuscaloosa, Alabama. "I came to Nashville [eighteen years ago]," she recalls, "to get some rapport with my mother." She was sixteen at the time. "I graduated from high school when I was fifteen. [I wanted] to be a juvenile probation officer. . . . I had to do a psychology thesis and I decided to do it on musicians and I started hangin' around on Lower Broad

Celinda Pink / Photo by Dennis Carney

. . . and just started singin'. Used to on Sixth Avenue, where the bus station was, used to be a couple of tiny little honky-tonks—hole-in-the-walls, actually, and I think the one I started in may have seated twenty people. I just started sittin' in with the band. I knew two songs, 'Ode To Billy Joe' and 'Me And Bobby McGee.' The name of the place was Tiger's Hideaway. It was a wild place. About every night there'd be two or three women on the bar strippin' and there was winos layin' around and I remember the lady that owned it, to get people to come in, she'd stand in the doorway and turn around and lift her dress up. It was wild. I didn't know if it was a brothel or a club.

"Now these clubs, it wasn't as if one was better than another because none of them paid. It was all tips, you worked for tips only but there was a lot of people there.

"When I got there it was about a year after the Opry had moved and the people were still comin' down there. [Lower Broad] was still real popular and the tourists were in the majority. The media is always talking about how rough Broadway is, and the deal is . . . it's nowhere near as rough as it was when I first started goin' down there. What was goin' on was, the lovers, muggers, and thieves were the minority and the tourists were the majority, and now it's the other way around, so you're more aware of what I call the back alley doin's than you were when it was a lot of tourists.

"Because back when I was goin' there there'd be eight hookers on every corner, pimps everywhere, drug dealers everywhere, robbers, and then when everything changed they sorta stood out. But now you don't see any hookers down there but you still see your little robbers and your little con artists, you know that kind of thing."

Many country artists, when they start their careers, have concrete dreams they pursue with energy and confidence. Celinda came from a different angle.

"Actually, I was very young and totally in the dark. I didn't know what I was doing. As I said, when I started I only knew two songs, and then I started learning more and more songs, and then I started playing guitar, writin' songs, and then I picked up the bass, started playin' bass. I had several different bands; I always was the leader of the band. Started off with a country band, then I went to an outlaw type band, and then I went to a rock band, and then I went to a blues band. But I've always had great players. No matter what kind of music I had in my band we always drew the biggest crowds."

The places she played read like a what's what on Lower Broad. "[I played at] all of them. I played at The Turf. I played at Music City Lounge, Tootsie's, Demon's Den when it was there. I played at Merchant's when it was a dump. [Merchant's today is a successful yuppie restaurant.]

"Matter of fact, I lived at Merchant's, upstairs, and played downstairs; and The Wheel, when it was down there. Just every single club there was, I played it."

Since Celinda was the biggest draw on Lower Broad, she always was in demand.

"That's the thing with me, I always been lucky. One club would offer me more money, or a better deal of some kind, little fringe benefits here and there. . . . ''

Obviously, by then she had progressed beyond the strictly-for-tips phase of her career.

"But I'm a very loyal person. One club I played three years, then I got bored with it and started playin' next door. Cuz on that street every club—it's like the twilight zone. You walk in one club and there's one atmosphere, certain type of people, then you can walk out the door, go next door, and it's just like walking into a brand new world.

"Like there's a club down there now called Diamond in the Rough, it's got valet parking. It's all real clean and they sell, you know, steaks and stuff like that, and the people that go in there have on suits and the women are all, like, models and stuff. And right next door to that, you'd think you died and went to wino heaven."

And when did she begin to think that maybe there was a recording career in her future?

"That's been a dream for . . . ten years. Everybody in the music business would of course wanna be a star, or have records. A lot of times I thought it was never gonna happen. But I never expressed that to anyone. I was always positive . . . to other people. 'Oh yeah [I'd say], it's gonna happen, don't worry about it.' Cause people would say, 'Well, when are you gonna do a record?' and I'd say, 'Well, one day,' and then they'd come back five years later and say, 'Are you *still* down here?'

" 'Yeah, I'm still down here.'

" 'Made any records?'

" 'Not yet.' ''

At this point she laughs a little laugh, and you get the

idea that there's a lot of pain associated with playing tiny clubs for tiny money just a dozen blocks away from where the big dollar deals are being made on Music Row. Journalists may be impressed by the art of the struggling blues and country singers, but I have never heard of a real performer who would rather perform his or her music for fifty dollars a night than perform the same music for five thousand dollars a night.

"I remember one night there were limousines parked on both sides of the street . . ." and she started reeling off the names of famous country singers who had come down to see her.

Then she mentioned the record producers who would make the short journey downtown to catch her act. "But they'd never do nothin'," she recalled, ruefully, showing just how long those twelve blocks can be when you've got dreams.

She knows that people in business who came down to see her thought they were just catching a great white blues singer, but like many great singers she stands ready to sing any kind of song she needs to to get a shot at making records.

"What these people cannot understand is that I played country music for years. I mean I knew every Patsy Cline, every Dolly Parton, every Willie Nelson [song] and I still do. And I still sometimes sing Ernest Tubb, Loretta Lynn— of course I always had a bluesy voice because I've had a lot of *pain* in my life, I can't help but have this kind of voice, but I can do a Koko Taylor song and growl with the best of them and then turn around and be smooth as silk like Patsy Cline."

Now the music world has plenty of white blues singers who believe their life has given them the right to sing the blues, but Celinda Pink doesn't have to display her credentials for anybody.

"My first blues experience [occurred when] I was five years old. And I was being adopted and I was in the courtroom. I can remember back to two years old and of course my mother and father were [laughs] rather violent with each other and most of my childhood experience from two years old to six years old were very traumatic memories.

"I realized I was being given to someone else. My family was leaving. My father was sitting in handcuffs, for what reason I don't know, all upset, and my mother was sitting there beaming, because this is what she wanted to do, and I stood up in the chair and I told my mother, 'If you will not leave me, I'll sing you a song,' and I performed 'Jesus Loves Me' in the courtroom. I guess that would have to be my first sad experience that really stands out.

"I was adopted by some people that I did not care for, and I think the feeling was mutual. They adopted me because my little sister was so attached to me that they just had to take me [when they took her]. And I overheard the lady say that to someone on the phone—I was about six—and I had a lot of problems. I cried a lot. The teachers would say, 'You gotta come and get her, she just won't stop cryin'.'

"And then my mother would pop up out of the blue and it was just like . . ." Here she pauses for several deep breaths because the tears are at the edge of her eyelids and she's not six years old anymore. She bites the tears back and continues. "Anyway, my mother would pop up in my life here and there and it was just traumatic. I guess these people probably didn't know what they were doin' to me but they were totally scarrin' me for life.

"And then I started gettin' swapped back and forth between my mother and my adopted parents. I'd go stay with my mother for a year and then her husband would decide that I was a problem and they'd send me back [to her adoptive parents] and finally I started running away from home and eventually they finally put me in reform school which was the best thing that ever happened to me."

Stop for a second and imagine a life so miserable that reform school was the best thing that ever happened to you.

"I only had to stay nine months but I spent three years

[in reform school] because I was finally somewhere where I was secure.

"I don't think I could sing this way had I not experienced what I did with all these people. 'Cause everybody in my life, with the exception of the people at reform school, just totally scarred me.

"I had a nervous breakdown when I was sixteen and I spent some time in a mental institution because of it. And [takes a deep sigh] couple of suicide attempts and it was all over the mother thing. Course I have a rapport with her now and I've forgiven her but it still hurts, you know, even at this age.

"Then, you know, I had missed out on the love thing for so long that when I got out of reform school and came to Nashville I married . . . a *horrible* person. He was very abusive mentally and physically. That's my son's father. I just sorta snatched the—lookin' for love, only it wasn't love. I seem to attract these guys that see the vulnerability in me.

"I didn't know my father very well. He was always in prison. The few times he was out I saw him but—my father's dead now but I was very close to him for some reason.

"I got out of that marriage," she continued. "Then got into another relationship that was just about the same as that one and then come Pete who at first seemed to be a very nice person and then he turned out to be a control freak. It's like I say, I sort of attract these people [that] see the emotional problems I have and they prey on that. Luckily here recently I have purchased a book that's called 'Women Who Love too Much,' which I would like to dedicate my next album to because I think that book is gonna help me a lot.

"I've been by myself for four years now because Pete scarred me so much on this man thing that I'm scared to death of 'em. As far as being serious. You know, I date [laughs]."

Celinda graduated from high school at the age of fifteen, a rare thing even for people who have their lives all together. For Celinda to have done this in spite of her emotional problems seems phenomenal.

"I think school is what kept me alive," she said. "I was very intelligent, and I was generally the teacher's pet . . . I just had an ability that was beyond normalcy, I guess you can say. It was like a place where I could prove myself and gain respect and pats on the back. I loved it because I felt achievement there.

"When I went to reform school the highest grade was third grade. There was a hundred girls there and most of them could not even read. [I know] 'Cause I used to test them, that was my job. . . . It was against the law for me not to go to school and they couldn't hire a bunch of teachers specifically for me so [after third grade] they used to unlock the gate for me every morning and I went to regular school and then they would unlock it in the afternoon [so I could get back into the reform school]. This was in Birmingham.

"That too was another painful experience because I did very well as far as the teachers go but the other students [in the regular school] did not accept me because I was in reform school. The bus stopped right in front of it [so the girls on the bus knew, and they'd say] 'Well, there's that delinquent' when actually I had it more together than most of them. You know, they were all doin' drugs, stuff like that, and I was just tryin' to get through school.

"I was editor of the [school] newspaper, I did manage to get that.

"People just don't realize what they do to you when you're a child; they don't realize how bad they can hurt you. This will never go away. This will be with me forever.

"So when people ask me, 'Well how do you get this pain in your voice?', it's 'cause it's in my heart. You know, the pain is really there. It's a fact. It's not contrived." She laughed, a quick, one-syllable chuckle that had little to do with happiness.

So how did her trip to Nashville come about?

"My mother lived here and I wanted to be around her.

Of course my probation officer—I was on probation when I got out of reform school—would not let me stay with her, [she said that my mother] was not fit, even though I was sixteen. And I [started] living as an adult. I was living at the YWCA and I was gettin' a rehabilitation check; college was paid for—I didn't pay for nothin'. Everything was paid. And that was another bad experience 'cause, you know, I had been locked up in reform school all this time. I didn't go to the prom, and I didn't go skatin' on Friday night and all the little things that teenagers are supposed to do, so I was just wild when I got out [of reform school], and what was bad about me goin' to college was that here I am, sixteen years old, and these people are—there's a lot of difference between sixteen and eighteen. So *they* didn't accept me. 'Oh, here's this smart-aleck kid here.' And I was, you know, somewhat immature. I was streetwise from what I had learned in reform school from the different girls, but I was lonesome, too. I was sad, because I had not had a life. I didn't have a childhood. I just merely *survived* through those years.''

So she went to the University of Tennessee in Nashville [now a part of Tennessee State University] for awhile.

Then came those eighteen years of singing down on Lower Broadway, before, finally, as the silly media cliche goes, she was ''discovered.''

''My manager [to be] had a friend who was a songwriter, and she just happened to be walkin' downtown one night and we had the door [to the club] open and she heard me and she came in and stayed all night. She called my [future] manager Buzz Ledford on the phone and says, 'You got to come down here and you're not gonna believe what you're gonna hear. This woman is awesome.'

''So he came down the next night and for about a year he was there every night. He was telling me he'd like to manage me and all this, and we didn't sign any kind of contract, it was an oral thing, you know, and I honored my end and he has honored his end and I've just recently finally signed a contract with him.

Celinda Pink / Photo by Sharon Pennington

"He just knocked around town trying to get me a [record] deal and everybody was like, 'Well she's just too blues. She's not a country singer.' "

A quick note here about the Nashville music scene: every so often a new performer will appear on the pop scene who paid his or her dues in Nashville without getting a record deal. And the media in covering the performer's story will spin it from the viewpoint of, "Nashville is too narrow and countrified to know a good pop talent when they hear it."

That's unfair. The major record labels are not headquartered in Nashville, they are headquartered in New York or L. A., and the executives in those towns either carry around their stereotype of Nashville as a strictly country town or don't want to see a rival pop scene grow up in Nashville. So Nashville record executives know that on the whole there is no sense attempting to develop pop acts in Nashville because they will get no support from the pop promotion and marketing divisions of their labels in New York or L. A.

During Buzz Ledford's rounds of the major record companies in Nashville he might have run into several record executives who were impressed by Celinda, but as long as they considered her a blues act, they had no way to market or promote her, and therefore no good reason to sign her.

"He went around for seven years trying to find me a record deal," she continued. "At the time I met him, he was not with any record company, and then he went to work for Airborne [a small independent record label that had a short existence during the eighties]. He later went to work for Step One and told Ray, 'You gotta hear this girl sing,' and he brought Ray to hear me. Ray liked [me] and I got the deal."

"Ray" is Ray Pennington, a music business veteran who runs one of only two successful independent record labels in Nashville, Step One Records. Pennington launched this label a number of years ago and at first kept it going selling albums on old favorites like Ray Price. But Pennington, who has written numerous hits and produced hit records on

artists like Waylon Jennings, wanted to fight the big boys
in the realm of contemporary country.

Pennington began his career in the record business perhaps four decades ago working for Sid Nathan's successful
King Records in Cincinnati. His skills in singing, producing, and songwriting have often tended toward the bluesy
side, so it's not surprising that he fell in love with the music
of Celinda Pink.

The fact is, country and blues are opposite sides of the
same coin, namely, the music of poor southern people.
Back in the first half of the twentieth century they may have
segregated the people of the south by race, but they never
completely segregated the music styles which have always
influenced each other.

"What people don't understand," Celinda tried to explain, "to me I'm a country singer. I love country music.
The heartfelt [feeling] makes it sound like the blues but it's
really not, it's truth, it's real. . . . When I'm singing a song,
any song, whether it be Patsy Cline, or a Celinda Pink song,
it's like I'm puttin' on a play. I am in that situation, at that
moment. And when that song's over and I start another
song, that's a totally different mood.

"I play five and a half hours a night and hold a crowd,
and I do 95 percent of the singin'. Generally when I go see
a woman sing, I can only listen for a little while, and then
I gotta go.

"I mean I have done songs and seen men cry their eyes
out, and then I've seen couples fight! Like I'll sing a certain
song and it's like the wife is sittin' there and all of a sudden
[laughs] she's punchin' her husband. 'Yeah!' [says the
wife] 'That's how you act! Un-huh! See that?'

"I mean, I've seen this happen. And I've had people tell
me, that's went through divorces, that said, if it weren't for
my music, they'd of went nuts.

"Because I write cocky stuff. It's like when I write . . .
this sounds so contradictory, I think this might be my alter
ego who writes my songs, but, I write songs that do not
put women in a 'poor pitiful me' bag. It's like, 'You're

gonna run around on me? Fine. I'm gonna run around on you.' It's like a rebellious type thing, it's not about being sad because this person has left, although I do have a few songs that are sad. But I've never recorded them and I probably never will.''

Celinda Pink is a tough, resilient child of the streets who has fought hard to bridge the huge gap that separates the hardscrabble grit of Lower Broad from the glamor of Music Row.

''So I dedicated my first album to a guy named Pete, who I lived with for seven years, and it was a very [sighs] emotional relationship. It was like mental abuse to the max . . . I was addicted to this guy. I need to come up with a word for it, or a group session for it [laughs].''

After her breakup with Pete, is there more blues in Celinda's future?

''In the past,'' she said, ''if I'd break up with somebody, two weeks later I'd a throwed myself into another relationship, I guess because I felt I needed this love and security. But this time, after Pete, I'm giving myself time. I got a wall up right now and when I get it together in myself, *then* I'll find someone. Till then I don't want a relationship because I am not stabilized personally to handle a relationship. I'll just attract the same kind of dude [laughs]. It never fails.''

So she focuses on her career. The late Conway Twitty used to talk about how glamor in show business is only make believe. If the glamor of the hit-making artist who plays before thousands of adoring fans every night is make believe, imagine how funky life must be in the tiny, noisy, smoky clubs of Lower Broad.

''The strange thing about Lower Broadway to me is that . . . I'm working in a club that seats maybe thirty people but I usually draw between fifty and a hundred in there, especially on the weekend, and I look around the room and it's like, a melting pot, just so many different kinds of people . . . there might be a guy sittin' over here that looks like he's probably drivin' a Jaguar. And then sittin' at the table next to him is a guy who doesn't have a home.

"There's college students in one corner, there's army boys in another corner, and there's a seventy-five or eighty-year-old man and wife in another corner, and they're all diggin' this music.

"How do I explain this? On Broadway you have a tip jug. Everybody has a tip jug. And now they pay you twenty-five dollars a night plus your tips. And I've had people give me a hundred dollar tip for one song. And that was cool. Evidently they could afford it. But I think the most touching thing—two times this happened, in two different ways.

"There's like a wino standing outside and they won't let him in the bar. But he walks in, and he puts, I'll bet three or four pennies in my tip jug, and that meant more to me than any hundred dollar tip I've ever gotten. This man walked in there and gave me everything he had.

"And then there was this little guy—he was a shoeshine guy. He come in and says, 'Celinda, I don't have any money, but I'll shine your shoes for free, 'cause you're just so great.' And while I was performing, he was shinin' my shoes . . . those are touching things I'll never forget.

"I've had several other what we call winos downtown. I really hate usin' that word, but for people to understand that's the word I have to use. But I have had some very touching moments with these people.

"I had this one lady come in and she just went nuts over my music and, first she was giving me money, and I guess she must have run out of that. Then she started giving me her hair barretts, and then she gave me her scarf. She gave me her coat, her shoes, and then she handed me her driver's license. Of course I gave it all back to her [saying], 'Look, I appreciate the fact that you like this music so much, but I don't want your license, I don't want your clothes. Thank you. Let me buy you a beer.'

"[laughs for a few moments] I've had some strange tips. I've actually had someone come in and give me a *water-*

melon. This one girl gave me a twenty-pound sack of potatoes.

"I'll be singin' and suddenly see this grown man cryin' like a little baby. I guess it's because people can feel this music, I mean, when they come down there to hear us play, they really hear it."

When the hot summer sun sinks on Lower Broadway, and the neon begins to peek through the haze, pickers tune their guitars and the music begins to pour out the doors of the clubs. Then the locals find their seats, and before long the air is close and fragrant with the smell of cigarette smoke, sweat, and perfume. Another night begins for Celinda Pink, who often works among friends.

"Most of them are homeless. They're very colorful characters. A lot of people don't realize that because I guess they're afraid they might get their hands dirty. But I've been around 'em for years and they're really basically very good people. Some of them are that way [homeless] by choice. They just don't like the business world. Like this one judge, he was a judge here in Nashville for years, and when he died—this was in the paper—this man had over a million dollars in the bank. But he lived like he didn't have a penny, this man slept on the concrete. But he just couldn't stand it anymore and he chose to live that way.

"This one guy, he walks around and he's got a Tennessee [license] tag on his chest. He used to sleep on top of Tootsie's, that was his home and he was very protective of the roof of Tootsie's Orchid Lounge. We called him 'Cityview' because he lived on top of Tootsie's. I don't know if they [the people who worked at Tootsie's] were aware of it or not, but everybody else was. [Laughs]. He was wild."

And what does Celinda Pink hope will happen to her?

"I want to, of course be a star, be famous, and I want to use my experiences . . . I've noticed a lot of stars, they deny a lot of things, and everybody knows it's true, but that's not what I want to do. I want to tell the truth. People need to know the truth. And if it's not a pretty story, so what. There's a lot of ugly stories in this world, and they need to be told so you can help people, especially young people. And also to let people know they're not alone, and there is hope."

And how will Celinda Pink's life change if she finally finds success on Music Row?

"I've thought about that a lot. Should I be highly successful naturally I'd be wealthy. I'm sure I'll gain a lot of what they call smiling faces. But I'm aware of that. I have a perception about that because I've been around the world twice on one little block right here in Nashville. You can't con me. I might let you think you are but you're not.

"Hopefully I'll be happy [laughs a happy laugh as she thinks about it]. I know you can't buy happiness, but then I'm not so sure about that, maybe you can."

When her first album, "Victimized," came out during the first part of '93, major publications gave her wonderful reviews. That kind of approval comes as a shock to someone used to being kicked around by the established world.

"When you've been where I've been you're almost in a thing where you feel like you don't deserve great things being said about you because you've been through so much *crap.* I find it amazing, and I've got nothing but rave reviews. I almost feel like Alice in Wonderland. Dumbfounded maybe. But wow, thanks.

"Nothing has ever been easy for me in music, and this thing that's happening now is not gonna be easy."

She's right about that. Step One Records is a successful record label headed by a wise old music veteran and staffed by competent professionals. But it is not a "major" record label, and in country music the major market radio stations seem to hate to play independent product.

Spokespeople for these stations will deny that they discriminate against small record labels. "If they give us good product we'll play their records," cry program directors, but the fact is, Step One already has one hit artist who sells hundreds of thousands of albums and gets solid play on the country video shows. Clinton Gregory is a country star, and yet he cannot get a top twenty chart single because too many big city country stations will not give him a shot at their markets.

We won't speculate at this time on the reasons for this problem. We'll just conclude by saying that as tough as Celinda Pink has had to be to survive the bad experiences in her life, that's how tough she'll have to be as she continues her long quest for success in the capricious world of commercial country music.

4

Dolly Parton

OF ALL THE FEMALE SINGERS IN COUNTRY MUSIC NONE has had a bigger impact than Dolly Parton.

No novelist could have created Dolly Parton. The only person on this entire earth with the imagination to create a person like Dolly is Dolly herself.

There are those who might think that Dolly hit her heights as a recording artist more than a decade ago when she made her successful switch from country to pop and then to movie stardom. But those people don't understand that Dolly Parton is an original. In country music, artists who turn their back on country music generally are never forgiven by their country fans. They regard it as a rejection of themselves and their culture, a case of somebody "gettin' above her raisin'."

When Dolly went pop, she went pop with all her heart, right down to the management, production, promotion, and redo of her physical image. Dolly does not do things halfway.

And yet, I believe, it was a given among country fans, in their heart of hearts, even if they weren't saying so, that whenever Dolly decided she wanted to come back, they would embrace her with their welcoming arms again. And of course, she did come back to country, so naturally, even those who followed her closely would swear that she'd never *really* been away.

Actually, the country industry owes a tremendous debt to Dolly. At a time when much of America still had very little respect for country music and the culture it represented, Dolly Parton, with her songs and her movies, made them respect her. They could not dismiss her as simply another hillbilly with a set of pipes. Even as they made jokes about her physical assets, she won them over with her sweetness and her talent. Many of today's country fans took their first steps toward country music by falling in love with the music and screen persona of Dolly Parton.

After more than three decades of Dolly Parton on the country scene—that's right, three decades (she started young)—her "Slow Dancing With The Moon" album was certified gold after only five months on the album charts.

It's nearly impossible not to be in awe of her talent, and her character, even if you work in the music industry, as does *Billboard* columnist Ed Morris. He has followed her for many years and has this to say about Dolly:

"Dolly will survive forever . . . she has this great gift of being as much of a sellout as she wants to be to male fantasies and at the same time being very much into what women have suffered and had to endure.

"The same woman who wrote 'Romeo,' which is a pandering song if I ever heard one, also wrote 'To Daddy,' which I think is just a gripping, gripping song about how a devoted woman will put up with it for so long and then eventually goes over the edge and that's it. I think Dolly still has worlds to explore."

I mentioned in a previous chapter that Dolly was motivated and focused and made her first commercial forays to Nashville in her early teenage years. How focused was she? The day after she graduated from Sevier County High School, she moved to Nashville. The date was June 22, 1964.

And she announced, both at her high school graduation

Dolly and Porter Wagoner ham it up.

and over the local radio station, that she intended to move to Nashville and make it in the world of big league show business. Obviously Dolly was not nursing fears that she might fail in her quest to become a star and come crawling back to Severville in a year or two, broken in spirit. She was all of eighteen years old when she, her uncle (and manager) Bill Owens, Owens' wife and their baby moved into a house close to the Tennessee State Fairgrounds.

Her early achievements included recordings of her songs by other country artists and several releases of her own on Fred Foster's Monument Records with minor success. The key to her career, however was a tall, lanky country singer from West Plains, Missouri, named Porter Wagoner.

In recent years the major book publishers of New York have discovered country music and published numerous biographies of country stars. One of the finest biographies ever written about country music, however, published in 1992 by Nashville's Rutledge Hill Press, (best known for H. Jackson Brown's big-selling *Life's Little Instruction Book*) is *A Satisfied Mind, The Country Music Life of Porter Wagoner*. The writer is Steve Eng, a man of talent and integrity.

Naturally Steve goes into some detail about Dolly, who, conversely, played an important part in Porter's career. He described Bill Owens' role in his niece's early career as being, "rather an East Tennessee equivalent of Ethel Gumm, who flogged her Gumm Sisters mother-daughter act down the yellow brick road through the portals of Hollywood. The youngest, Frances Gumm, became Judy Garland. Like Judy, Dolly had no choice but to become a star, a child-chattel to her show-biz destiny." It must be remembered that Dolly, in the years of her management contract with Uncle Bill, was, like Judy, very young. As she matured, she gradually took control of her career as few females in show business have ever done, but that was later, much later.

Eng devotes a substantial portion of his book to the relationship between Porter and Dolly, and well he should, because their few years together as music collaborators were among the most important in their lives. Their story is especially fascinating because while Dolly's ambition was to become one of the major figures in America's entertainment industry, Porter longed for nothing more than to continue on as a communicator of traditional country music. Both of them were, and are, extremely successful in accomplishing their goals.

Before Eng describes their meeting, he offers some interesting views of Dolly's background:

"Dolly has made unsettling statements to the press concerning the cold, hard facts of mountain life. Connie Merman, in the *Official Dolly Parton Scrapbook*, quotes her as saying she has seen many strange goings-on and knows where there are many shallow graves in the mountains. To

Lawrence Grobel of *Playboy*, Dolly admitted that while the kids never learned from their parents where babies came from, their uncles and cousins shared their feelings on the topic down in the barn and, 'as soon as we'd get a chance, we'd try it.' Robert K. Oermann from the *Tennessean* asked Dolly about an abused-woman lyric ('What Is It, My Love'), and she condemned the 'macho, redneck attitudes' of her father, her brothers, 'and a lot of my people,' and said she wouldn't recommend anyone marrying one of her brothers. 'Now I love 'em to death,' she says, 'but this song was inspired by my family and how some of 'em treat their women.' The stories of Dolly being beaten for having painted her lips with Merthiolate or for making fake eyebrows with burnt matches are stock Parton legends by now, as are all the mentions of the children's bed-wetting, from sleeping all crammed together. In her song 'Evening Shade,' Dolly has a little girl in an orphanage whipped by a matron with a razor strap for wetting her bed, then some other kids get kerosene and wait till the matron is asleep and burn the place down.''

Back in 1967 Porter Wagoner was one of country music's brightest stars. Although his RCA recordings were moneymakers, and often high chart records, he was best known for his weekly syndicated half-hour television show. His show always featured a song or two from a guest star, the lively picking of his band, and the vocals of his girl singer, ''Miss Norma Jean,'' who had a number of hits on RCA herself.

And then Norma Jean decided to get married and leave the show. Porter needed a replacement and decided on Dolly, who had made herself visible with several appearances on local and syndicated TV shows.

Probably because Porter does not qualify as a great singer, and because of his sequined suits and down-home stage persona, he is vastly underrated as a country artist. Unlike most country artists of the sixties and early seventies, he had no desire to toy with the pop side of country music. No doubt he heard Dolly's crystal-clear Appalachian

Dolly and Porter on their Comin' Home *television show.*

voice and it struck a chord in him. He left a call at Monument Records requesting that Dolly meet with him, and when she did, he asked her if she would like to be part of his show.

To Dolly, like so many other country folks in America in those days, Porter was a great star, and he was a friend who visited the house of her family on TV once a week during her growing-up years. Dolly took the job, and soon it was obvious that the two made a perfect musical match. In late 1967 they had their first duet single, ''The Last Thing on My Mind,'' which became a top ten record. At the age of twenty-one, Dolly was well on her way toward realizing her dream of becoming a country star.

Over the next six years Porter and Dolly became the hottest duo in country music. When they weren't on the road, which they usually were, they were in the studio, or writing together, or otherwise focusing on their joined musical careers.

Over the years many people have speculated that Porter's preoccupation with Dolly's career was due to an obsessive love affair. A more likely speculation would be that Porter was so stimulated by Dolly's talent and potential that he was motivated to spend hundreds of hours in the studio working on the recordings of Dolly, and of Porter and Dolly, to the detriment of Porter's solo recordings.

This period was a great period of growth for both of them. Porter Wagoner, hillbilly singer, became Porter Wagoner, producer extraordinaire, building a studio, learning technology, writing some of his best songs, and fighting corporate battles with RCA. Dolly began this period under the thumb of Porter and gradually asserted more and more independence until finally, in 1974, she split from Porter, first as a road performer, then corporately, and finally, completely.

It was rough for Porter. Country music had by then left the rhinestone suits and songs of self-pity behind, along with many of Porter's peers. Thanks to his professional growth, largely due to the Dolly association, he had enjoyed some of his greatest successes. It was tough for him both professionally and emotionally to make the adjustment. But over the years, he did, and he seems to have become the successor to Roy Acuff as the flag carrier for a mightier-than-ever Grand Ole Opry.

The transition was difficult for Dolly too. It's always easy, after the fact, to assume that a great star like Dolly knew for sure that she was on her way to bigger and better things. When she split from her mentor she may have known where she wanted to go, but she certainly did not know how she was going to get there. There were a lot of mistakes to be made, and plenty of worry on the way to the top. One of her friends and employees during that time of transition was veteran hit songwriter Frank Dycus.

"If the whole world was like Don Williams and Dolly

Parton,'' Dycus is fond of saying, ''there'd be no more poverty, no more war, and no more bad things happening.''

What does she mean to country music?

''To me she's the mountain that everybody else has gotta climb. If you're gonna be a girl star you're gonna have to go all the way past Dolly and that's virtually impossible. Because she's done it all. She's a huge publisher, she's a huge writer, she's a huge artist, she's a huge actress, she's a huge businesswoman, so that's a big mountain.''

The way Dycus first met Dolly is reminiscent of a time when Nashville's Music Row was a much folksier place, before the business world gobbled it up. Today Music Row is owned by about two dozen corporate entities separated by high, invisible fences and linked by voicemail and occasional table-hopping at Mario's. But twenty years ago Music Row was actually a neighborhood where neighbors talked to each other over back fences.

''I was writin' for Pete Drake on Eighteenth and she was of course two doors down at Owepar [Porter and Dolly's publishing company]. It just started out hollerin' 'Hi,' you know, when she'd come in over there at Owepar, and she'd holler 'Hi' over there at us, we'd be sittin' out on the porch tryin' to come up with a hit idea.

''I think it was 1970, Porter cut one of my songs called '40 Miles From Poplar Bluff,' and then she did a duet with him on it, and it was on the 'Album of the Year' [in] 1970. So then, I was at the session, which was very rare. Larry Kingston and I had been writin' together for a couple of years and gettin' a lot of songs cut, and somebody come into the session—I believe it was Dave Kirby [one of Nashville's finest studio guitar players and songwriting talents of the time] and said, 'Who wrote that song?'

''And Porter said, 'Larry Kingston,' and Dolly jumped up and said, '*and Frank Dycus*.'

''[Then she turned around and looked at me and said] 'Don't that make you mad?' ''

Songwriters frequently don't get much credit for the

songs they write, and Dolly was voicing her sympathy for a fellow songwriter.

"I said, 'Well, you know. . . .' It kind of embarrassed me, I was scared to be at the session anyway and intimidated by all of it and Dolly turned around to Bob Ferguson [producer and/or overseer of many Porter and Dolly records] and said, 'Put his name on that record first.' And I just got the feelin' that night that I would spend a lot of time with Dolly Parton and I came home and told my wife that. You know, I said, 'I just met a woman I'm gonna spend a lot of time with,' oh yeah, she didn't understand it and sure enough a year or so later we [meaning Pete Drake] sold the publishing company to Owepar—Louis Owens, her uncle [and business associate], bought my publishing company and signed us as writers, me and Kingston.

"I started out [at Owepar] as a songplugger and writer and . . . at the time it all ended, when her and Porter separated their enterprises, I was runnin' Fireside Studio and Owepar Publishing Company and producin' records and bein' a songplugger and songwriter for Dolly.

"I worked with her for four, maybe five years and I never once in those four years saw her upset, mad, you know, she always treated me like a member of her family and she was always just as good 'n kind to me as she could possibly be and still is after all these years.

"I was one of the very few people that worked for both of them [after the split]. He had his band and his people and she had her band and her people . . . and I tried to divide my loyalty among two people who at the time were having difficulty gettin' along together."

It must have been frustrating, and a little frightening, to be working for them at the time.

"To be honest with you [their breakup] came as a total shock to me. I knew they were havin' difficulties because you know she had formed her family band and gone on the road, and Don Warden [Porter's steel player and right-hand man] had left Porter to manage her . . . you know, I was more or less left in the dark about what was going on

Dolly with Ricky Van Shelton.

around me until the day the curtain fell. That was, I mean, absolute devastation to me.

"The best four or five years I spent on Music Row was spent with her organization. There was never any intimidation. They just let us do whatever we wanted to do. I told them I wanted to bring somebody in, record them in the studio, we did it. No questions asked and no lookin' over your shoulder . . . If I wanted a raise I went to Louis and told him I wanted a raise and he went to Dolly and I got a raise."

Frank Dycus is a stocky country boy from Kentucky who looks a little bit like a troll, a man with a big heart, the kind of man people feel comfortable with, so it was inevitable that during a time of great stress Dolly would at least once confide in him.

"One night on the bus she was real upset and she talked to me about it. She didn't know what to do, didn't know where she was goin' and what was goin' on, and that was when I decided to do something about furtherin' her career. [At the time] she was playin' for thirty-five hundred dollars a night with her family band and she had just cut an album with them, and you know she wasn't sellin' that many albums, maybe a hundred and twenty, a hundred and thirty thousand."

Today those numbers are considered paltry in country music, but twenty years ago those were fairly good figures for most country artists. But Dolly was reaching out for superstardom, and she knew she had to achieve some sort of breakthrough, she just didn't know how.

"I compared her to Emmylou [Harris]. I said, 'You know Emmylou has had one single out or two singles and she's gettin' ten grand a night, and her record sales are already at two hundred thousand. It's marketing and it's management, something's missing.' I called Mary Martin [at Warner Brothers in New York] about what Emmylou was doin' [that made her so successful so quickly].

"She was a friend of mine and she was also a Dolly Parton fan. And Emmy had cut one of Dolly's songs. We

*Linda Ronstadt, Emmylou Harris, and Dolly at the
Country Music Awards in 1986.*

got to discussin' it and it was Mary's idea to put Dolly and
Emmy and Linda Ronstadt together and I followed up on
this end and . . . sent Dolly to California to meet 'em and,
you know, see what could be done. And I really think that
was the turnin' point in Dolly's career, to where she could
advance, get on the *Tonight Show*. Up to that point it was
like she was just bein' held back by Nashville.

"I saw things that very few people saw, or even pre-
tended to see. We were in St. Joseph, Missouri, one night
and I looked up and there were fifty or sixty black people
in the crowd. I had never seen that at a country show before
and I knew then that Dolly had the appeal to the masses
that we didn't know about. It was a matter of marketing."

Dycus is probably right that Dolly's contact with Emmylou Harris and Linda Ronstadt was the key to the Dolly
Parton explosion. Both of them had a strong California
base, and it must be remembered that at the time the New
York and California entertainment industry had little respect for anything that came out of Nashville. Nevertheless,

Dycus gives himself very little credit for her career successes and gives her tremendous credit for his.

"I've not had a rough time since my association with her, and up till that point it was starvation row."

Dycus feels that Dolly "apparently knew what she wanted to do [at the time of their conversation] because it wasn't long after that she disbanded the family band and went to L. A. and found her a new producer and started doin' what Dolly does today and that's exactly what Dolly wants.

"I think Dolly is super strong. She plans out things and then does it."

Evidently she does it right, because from the time she established her California connections until today, she has had the kind of success that has allowed her to follow her creative whims anywhere they carry her.

Many performers once seduced by Hollywood look back at their roots with some contempt, and would no more want to return to them than a major league pitcher would want to return to the rookie league team with which he started in professional baseball. But Dolly has proved, again and again, that she is one of a kind.

"I think probably you'll need to research this because this is just stuff that I've heard secondhand," Dycus said. "But I've heard, and I believe, that every child in Sevier County, Tennessee, who doesn't have breakfast at home can eat breakfast at school on Dolly Parton.

"And I also heard that every child in Sevier County, Tennessee, who doesn't have the money for lunch . . . can eat lunch on Dolly Parton. And I've also heard that every child in Sevier County who graduates from Sevier County High School gets a five hundred dollar check from Dolly Parton. And I've also heard that every child who is failing and has a buddy that helps them get through school, the buddy gets a thousand dollars. And I've also heard that if you enter college after graduating from high school, if you pass the college exam, you get another check from Dolly Parton for five hundred dollars. Now I don't know whether this is all true or whether it's hearsay or what, but if I was gonna bet money I would bet every bit of it's true.''

Now, think about this for a minute. Many show business personalities contribute money and effort to charitable causes. And many of them have publicists whose job appears to be making sure the public hears about what wonderful, charitable folks these people are. I haven't read about any of this stuff Dolly has done for Sevier County, have you?

Well, maybe it isn't true, right? Wrong. At a recent function I met a young lady who had just a short time ago graduated from the Sevier County school system, and she knows firsthand that at the very least most of Dycus's information is true.

Dolly Parton knew poverty in her childhood and decided to do something about it. And so she set up the Dollywood Foundation, aimed specifically at the folks back home, the people she left behind, but never really left behind. Not that it's a secret. It isn't, but neither is it a highly publicized gimmick to promote her public image.

''Dolly Parton flat takes care of people who need takin' care of,'' Dycus asserted. ''She made the statement over and over again, if she's got a dime, her family's got a nickel.

''Dolly was a magic person when she was born, and I think the magic has stayed with her through the years and I think the magic will stay with her right up to her last breath. You can be in the room with her and not even know she's in the room, but you'll know you're in the room with somebody special. You get that feeling, it's an aura, and then all of a sudden you look up and there's Dolly.

''Things mean a lot to Dolly. She's rebuilt the whole valley where she used to live in eastern Tennessee. Her brother built a house, school, church, it's all in one little valley over there, and it's like a one-room schoolhouse, a little bitty church with a church bell ... she calls it [the valley] her Tennessee mountain home. It's not built as a tourist attraction, it's not open to the public, it's ... her hideaway.''

Obviously Dolly is a woman who makes her dreams come true.

"Her dreams and your dreams. She'll make your dreams come true if you're a part of her family and you're a part of her organization. She gives her pickers points on an album. Now is that unbelievable?"

Points are percentages of the price of an album. Recording artists, producers, and managers fight hungrily with record labels for those points, which can represent hundreds of thousands of dollars to whoever owns them. Session musicians are generally paid a fixed fee for their work on a session, generally union scale or a multiple thereof if the musician is in great demand. It is almost unheard of for a performer to assign record royalties to musicians. Unlike many people, in or out of the music business, who believe record sales are simply a reflection of the talent of the featured artists, Dolly Parton knows that recording success is a collaborative effort featuring the talents of producers, engineers, songwriters, musicians, record promoters, radio station music directors; the list goes on and on. Dolly Parton knows about all of it because she's made it her business to know about all of it.

What is it about her that has allowed her to make the journey from the rocky valleys of her childhood to the top of the entertainment industry?

"I think," Dycus said, "it's that bubblin' over attitude of Dolly's. Like I said, I was with her for four or five years, I never saw her depressed except for that one night on the bus when she seemed confused and depressed and wore out with the road. Outside of that for five years she come in (every morning) just a-bubblin' over like, 'Which mountain do I climb today? Let me at it!'

"It's a gift of God. She was a gifted child and she turned into a gifted adult and she never forgot that she's got a gift."

Dolly Parton has created a bigger-than-life character of the same name. Dycus got just a tiny sample of what that means.

Kenny Rogers presents Dolly with the Special Lifetime Achievement Award.

"I ran out of Pete Drake's studio one night, running back to Fireside [Porter and Dolly's studio] cause we'd run out of tape and I'd run over [to Fireside] to borrow some. And I ran into Dolly behind the building in the parking lot and she didn't have on a wig. Or makeup, nothin'. She had on jeans and a T-shirt and I didn't recognize her. Didn't know who she was. And when her little ol' voice come out of that person, you know, with natural hair, no makeup... and she seemed real tiny, you know, compared to the way she normally seemed and I thought, 'My God, this is *Dolly...*'

"When her Uncle Louis couldn't make the road gigs then I'd go out, actin' as the road manager. [One night] I got the house to dim the lights on 'I Will Always Love You,' and at the end of it, just for a second, black 'em out. And I didn't know that Dolly was deathly afraid of the dark. And when she come back on the bus she didn't reprimand me [much]—cause she had apparently gone and found out who turned out the lights—she just said, 'I don't like that!' And it was just an absolute marvelous way to end the song. The people went wild and it scared Dolly to death."

Dolly, Dycus explained, gets involved with her people.

"See I had a real problem bein' able to sing my songs to people, and I also had a problem bein' able to talk to people in the music business. Really I was super intimidated by Nashville. Dolly just told me, 'You know you put your breeches on just like everybody else does, they put theirs on just like you do. You can just get up and pick your guitar up, you're a great writer, it don't matter if you sing out of meter, just sing your songs.' She gave me a lot of confidence that I didn't have."

After his apprenticeship under Dolly, Dycus's career really began to climb. George Strait and George Jones in particular have recorded one Frank Dycus song after another. He credits Dolly for giving him the confidence that has made the difference in his career.

"She made me feel good about myself all the time, not just once but every time I saw her," he explained.

Thousands of people write to Dolly for help and you can't be a sucker for everybody. Dycus recalled that "I remember one time she brought me a letter . . . told me to do something about it . . . from some woman in Oklahoma that said her kids were starvin' to death and didn't have clothes to wear and all that, and I got to lookin' at the letter and the sizes, you know, sixteen-year-old boy wears forty-eight waist jeans? These people are not starvin' to death, and I just kind of ignored the letter and went on."

He doesn't have an awful lot of communication with Dolly these days.

"I know I could if I wanted to, if I needed to. But I get messages from her every once in a while from other people, 'Tell Dycus I love him.' I'll tell you something really interesting. She cut one of my songs on her new album and I got a tape copy of it before it was ever mixed and I also got a note, with the tape, that said, 'Dycus, thank you very much, I love you, Dolly.'

"April a year ago I decided I was gonna start a publishing company with Warner Brothers. I was at the point where I was startin' a brand new career . . . I had planned for three or four months what I was gonna do, and I left a message to Dolly that I was wondering what the possibilities were that I could get back a bunch of old copyrights that she owned since '74."

Let me explain the gist of his request. During the time Frank Dycus worked for Dolly, she paid him to write songs for her, and then paid the studio and musician costs for making demo tapes on many of those songs. Dolly had therefore spent a lot of money on those songs and they added to the value of her publishing company. Now here was her friend, Frank Dycus, asking her to give these songs to him. That's not an unusual request, but the vast majority of publishers, noting how much the songs had cost them to acquire, would have refused, or at least demanded that the writer *buy* them back.

"I got a call from the people who run her publishing organization and they said Miss Dolly is gonna give you back sixty-somethin' copyrights.

"I said, well fine, I'll get a holt of the lawyers, get all the paperwork done and they said, no, that's not necessary, all you have to do is come out here and pick up the tapes and the contracts."

That's the kind of informal way of doing business that was once fairly common on Music Row, twenty years ago or more. But big business has pretty much taken over. The country boys have been replaced by carpetbaggers with sharp pencils, Tums, and Preparation H. Dolly is one of the few left who still treasures a time when friendship meant trust.

One of the reasons Porter and Dolly fought so hard after they broke up was the informal way they had arranged their business relationships. You may be certain that when Dolly makes a deal with a Hollywood studio her lawyers make sure that every *t* gets crossed and every *i* dotted. But that longing for the old, simpler days must be stronger in her than it is in most of us, so when old friend Frank Dycus wants his songs back he gets them back the simple, old-fashioned way, hand to hand, tapes and contracts. Of

*Dolly puts her hand prints on Star Walk at Fountain Square
in Nashville.*

course, it's also part of Dolly's shrewdness to know that
that's all that's legally necessary for the deed to get done.

"And I started a great publishing company with Warner
Brothers with that batch of songs," Dycus said. "I'll tell
you one thing, I've been here thirty-something years and
I've never had anybody give me one song back, much less
a whole catalog, until now. Thank you Dolly."

When Dolly went pop, much of the thrust of the media
hype asserted that she was turning her back on Nashville
for the presumably brighter lights of L. A. But Dycus said
that never happened.

"She's always had a Nashville base of operations. Don
Warden's office has always been here. Right now she keeps
a huge Nashville base of operations."

Her base, Twelfth Avenue South, one of the less glam-
orous Nashville locations, is a walled compound, sparsely

staffed, with offices, rehearsal rooms, and hallways lined with awards.

"It looks like the Alamo," Dycus observed. "You look up and you expect to see Davy Crockett standing on top of the wall."

Not a bad thought—a place for two American legends from the mountains of Tennessee.

5

Reba McEntire

FEMALE COUNTRY SINGERS HAVE A MUSICAL HERITAGE entirely different from male country singers. Here's what I mean:

Today's country explosion was created largely by male singers who sing like the guys who came before. We all know the bloodlines: Jimmy Rodgers to Lefty Frizzell to Merle Haggard to Randy Travis. Or, Jimmy Rodgers to George Jones and Vern Gosden to Sammy Kershaw.

Alan Jackson, Mark Chesnutt, John Anderson, Garth Brooks, Dwight Yoakam, Clint Black, George Strait—so many of them pay homage to the great country stars before them by the way they bend a note or phrase their lyric.

The same cannot be said of female country artists. There is no Kitty Wells style line. No Loretta Lynn line or Tammy Wynette line. Not even a Patsy Cline line, though some have tried. In fact, many people in the business have remarked that the present country explosion has yet to produce a single, certifiable female honky-tonk star.

Why? Does it have to do with the kinds of artists the labels are looking for? I don't think so because probably every A & R person who combs the clubs looking for the next female star would just love to come across the female counterpart to Randy Travis. So far it just hasn't happened, though there are a few out there who show promise.

Today's hit female artists in general come in two varieties: Rough and smooth. The rough ones have that jagged rasp to their voices, that cigarette and whiskey sound. Tanya comes to mind immediately, as do Michelle Wright and Wynonna. Many of them look back to black R & B singers for their vocal inspiration.

The smooth variety looks back to folky forebears like Judy Collins and Anne Murray, and also true Appalachian singers like the Carters. Some of the present ones include Mary-Chapin Carpenter, Suzy Bogguss, Kathy Mattea, and Dolly Parton.

But one female country singer stands by herself because she can sing any way she pleases anytime she pleases. That singer is the extraordinary Reba McEntire.

When Reba first started out at Mercury Records, many thought she would be that hard-to-find hard country girl singer. After all, she was a rodeo queen, and she looked country and acted country, and she sure sang country.

But so many of today's female country singers seem to have the urge to stretch themselves musically, perhaps because so many of them sing so well. And nobody sings better than Reba, so naturally over the years her musical adventures have taken her in many directions. The more successful she has become, the more control she has taken over her career, the more chances she has taken, the more ulcers she has given anxious promotion and marketing people until they began to realize that whatever she chooses to sing her fans will buy.

There used to be a studio in the wilderness just north of Nashville called Nugget. It was one of those studios where creative things happened. It was a great place to produce song demos and "spec" sessions—sessions done to get an artist a record deal—because it was reliable, and it was inexpensive. For example, about fifteen years ago, a producer named Brien Fisher cut a few songs there on a father/

Reba McEntire performs early in her career.

daughter singing act from Arkansas. The session helped them get their deal on tiny Ovation Records out of Glenview, Illinois, and within a year's time the Kendalls had the hottest country record in the country, "Heaven's Just a Sin Away."

Sometime in the mid-1970s Red Steagall went to Nugget to cut a few sides. Red is one of those Texas guys who made a great living touring the honky-tonks of Texas, where he was almost a legend. But Red never quite broke big on the national scene, although he had a fair number of national chart records.

At this particular time, the sides Red cut were not on himself, but on a girl from Oklahoma named Reba McEntire. According to Don Cusic in the biography, *Reba, Country Music's Queen*, Red then told Reba and her mother to go back home and forget about the session (at Nugget), while he went around trying to get a deal for her.

It doesn't matter how great you think your favorite country star is, the chances are good that when that artist first came to Nashville, he or she was turned down by most of the labels in town. Don Cusic said that Reba's tape was played all over Nashville and played for record executives who said that they did not need another female singer. Throughout the history of country music, women have been perceived as the primary buyers of records, and most women seemed to prefer listening to men. Why? Who knows. But because of that perception, it has always been terribly hard for a woman to get a country record deal. A typical ratio of men to women on a record label's country roster has been four or five men to every woman. Even today, there are record executives in Nashville who have had so little success with female artists that they would rather kiss a water moccasin than sign a girl singer.

Joe Light, Steagall's associate at the publishing company for which they were both working, took the tape to Mercury Records, and Glenn Keener, A & R man there at the time, liked the way Reba sang. Fortunately, the label was interested in signing a female singer at the time.

Today, Mercury Records is a busy place, the home of Kathy Mattea, Toby Keith, and Billy Ray Cyrus, but in those days Mercury was the stepchild of all the major label country divisions. Their mainstay was the Statler Brothers, and even the "Stats" were usually not monster record sellers. So having a deal on Mercury was not necessarily the best thing that could happen to an artist.

But Mercury was the label that wanted her, so in No-

Reba at FanFair in 1979.

vember of 1975 she signed with the label. She was a re-
markable singer and her label knew it. They released single
after single on her even though she did not get her first top
ten single until 1980 with ''(You Lift Me) Up To Heaven.''

Over the next three years her records were good and earned consistently decent chart positions, but her sales were still not kicking in and Mercury still did not have a solid reputation for hot-selling country albums. In 1983 she moved over to MCA Records. The executive who signed her at MCA was the redoubtable Jim Foglesong.

Foglesong has a reputation for integrity over the course of his long career in the record business that took him first to New York, where he worked for Columbia and RCA, then to Nashville, where he headed first Dot Records, then ABC, MCA, and Capitol. He was successful whatever label he ran, signing such notable future stars as Garth Brooks, George Strait, and Suzy Bogguss. He talked about bringing Reba to MCA Records.

"Irving Azoff [then California-based head of MCA Records and now the head of Giant Records], who was my boss at the time, called me and asked me if I would be interested in having Reba McEntire on the label. I said yes. She had just recorded two of my favorite records. I can't remember the second one but [the first] was called 'I'm Not That Lonely Yet.' Jerry Kennedy [a veteran, almost legendary producer] had had her on Mercury for several years with varying degrees of success. She had chart activity but I don't think anybody in the industry thought of Reba as being the great singer that she was, but suddenly . . . I think they were both number one records . . . boy, she got my attention and everybody else's.

"And I said, absolutely, I didn't know that she was available and he [Azoff] said, 'Well, I played tennis with Don Williams today.' "

This Don Williams is not the great country singer Don Williams. This Don Williams is Andy Williams's brother, who has managed Ray Stevens for years and also at the time managed the aforementioned Red Steagall, discoverer of Reba McEntire.

"Red was very active in the rodeo circuit," said Foglesong. "Reba is from a rodeo family. She used to perform in rodeos . . . actually when I met her she was married to a

Reba receives the TNN Viewers Choice Award.

rodeo star [Charlie Battles]. [So Azoff said] Well, call Don
Williams because she's about to sign with CBS.

"So I called Don, whom I knew quite well, and he said,
'Bill Carter [then her lawyer and later her manager] is flying around Canada right now carrying a draft of a CBS
contract. . . . You're gonna have to probably get on a plane
and go to Boise, Idaho, and meet Reba.' He said, 'We're
probably gonna go to CBS but they didn't give us everything we wanted, we're not totally happy,' something like
that, I can't remember the exact details. Well, I was on a
plane the next day and Don also flew up from L. A. and
met me, and we went to a rodeo, and heard Reba do her
show, saw Charlie compete, throwing a bull, whatever the
right expression is, and had dinner in what we were told
was one of the better restaurants in town, which was either
a Western Sizzler or Bonanza, that type of steakhouse, and
met with them, talked with them, had a wonderful
discussion.

"The first question I asked her was 'Why in the world
are you leaving Mercury, because they've been your label
for so long and Jerry is a great producer and I just love
these last two records you made.'

"And she just praised Kennedy to the skies, but she'd
been on the label for so long and [been] thought of in such
a stereotypical way that she really wanted to reach out and
do other things. And she felt like she should go to a place
where she could get a fresh start. Prior to her last two hit
singles on Mercury, Reba had been cutting what the industry calls 'work' records."

It might be well here to explain what a work record is.
To most fans a hit is a hit is a hit. If the Saturday morning
countdown says an artist's record has made it to the number
five position, we assume that means it is the fifth most
popular record in the country, but that's not always the way
it is.

When a record company puts out a single, it assigns in-
house promotion people and also a number of independent

Reba receives the Best Female Vocalist Award at the CMA Show in 1987.

record promoters to get that record as high on the charts as they can. The various charts (*Billboard, Radio and Records,* and the *Gavin Report* are three important examples) each have hundreds of radio stations that report to them, telling them how well each current record is doing. So the promoters contact all these reporting stations and try to get them first to play the record, then to advance the record up their charts or their rotation (many stations play records in light, medium, or heavy rotation). Ideally, when a record is moving nicely up the charts, most of the reporting stations will be moving the record up their charts more or less in sync so the record will not be peaking too early at some stations and dropping from some local charts even while it's still climbing in others.

When the stations perceive a certain record is a genuine hit, then the promoters have a fairly easy job. The conversation with the station sounds something like this:

Promoter: I'm callin' about Joe Blow's new single, "Heavenly Cowboy." You had it at number twenty seven last week. Where's it goin' this week?

Station Music Director: Goin' up five spots to number twenty-two.

Promoter: Aw, that's great Sam. That's pretty much the response we're gettin' from the other stations around the country. I think we've got a real hit on Joe, finally.

Station Music Director: Me too.

That's when you have a real radio hit. But then, sometimes the record's pretty good, not great, and then the promoter has to beg, whine, tell the music director how terribly important this is to the label or to his own job. In the past, money, drugs, or gifts were known to change hands to gain cooperation from important stations. This is a "work record," a record that requires a lot of begging or persuasion by promoters to get it up the charts. The presumption is that maybe the record wasn't all that great if the promoters had to work that hard. After all, the purpose of a country single is to sell country albums, and it takes a powerful single to make a big difference in album sales. Reba's Mercury singles were only beginning to make a sales impact.

"So with that in mind [Reba's disenchantment with Mercury] I did my best to tell her we'd love to have her [on MCA], and we'd work her product. Whatever I told her seemed to work because we did end up signing her."

Back in the seventies, when Reba first came on the scene,

*Reba and Lee Greenwood after a 1980s
Music City News Awards.*

there were only three or four female artists racking up substantial record sales. Today there are three times that many.
But Reba has them all beat in sales, with only Wynonna
in the same neighborhood. Her career is proceeding on

all fronts, and there are good reasons. Foglesong talked about them.

"Reba is extremely bright, and very ambitious, and willing to work as hard as it takes to achieve her goals. She's funny, reminds me a little of Loretta Lynn, Dolly Parton; these are people who have a God-given talent for saying the right thing at the right time, whether it's on the *Tonight Show* or in your office, they're sharp and funny and colorful.

"She's just a total entertainer and I admire her tremendously. She's obviously worked with choreographers and people . . . clothing her, makeup and hair, and all these things which an artist should really do, but a lot of them don't."

This is in sharp contrast to her early days when her image was that of the innocent girl in the rodeo clothes.

"She's a Barbara Mandrell type who's just got that killer instinct to be a star and to do great shows."

At her first meeting with Foglesong "[Bill Carter] was talking about using a British producer to do her first video [on MCA], the one that had just recently done one on Olivia Newton-John for about a hundred and ninety thousand dollars, and I'm sitting there [thinking] well how am I going to handle this, we don't spend that kind of money, particularly back then, for Nashville type videos . . . they had big, big plans back then. She definitely wanted to reach out into more of a nontraditional image, more pop influence." But like other successful stars, she would find a way to preserve her own style and identity no matter which way she went.

"One of the things that I spotted in Reba in her show at the rodeo out in Boise, she did a Patsy Cline medley, and when it first started I was thinking, oh no, not another Patsy Cline medley; it was kind of trite because so many people did that. Every lounge somebody [would do a Patsy Cline medley], but I'll tell you, she *killed* those songs. I've heard a lot of people do those and do them well but I don't think

anybody did them as well since Patsy did the originals.

"The voice and the interpretation, really understanding the songs, just killed me, and I really [had been] prepared to tune out that whole section of the show, once she started into 'Crazy,' or whatever song it was that she did."

During the earlier part of her career, Reba handled her recording situation the way most female artists did through the years. That is, she let her producer find the songs, then he would play them for her, and together they would decide which of these they would take into the studio. But in 1984, according to biographer Don Cusic, a change occurred.

As country as Reba is, most of her early years as a country singer were spent cutting what the country music industry called "middle-of-the-road" songs. These are generally love ballads and smooth uptempos that sound a lot like pre-rock and roll pop music and are maybe a step or two more interesting as records than the bland instrumentals they call elevator music.

Reba recorded so many of these songs because until the coming of Randy Travis, most country artists recorded these songs. The record companies perceived that radio wanted those kinds of songs to play for their older audiences on the way to and from work. One day in 1984, according to Cusic, Reba decided that she wanted to record songs that were more country. By that time Jimmy Bowen had succeeded Jim Foglesong at MCA and Bowen was known to be a very bright music man, so Reba went to Bowen to find out how to get songs she'd like better than those her producers had been bringing to her.

Bowen told her, sensibly enough, to go out and find them herself. Go call the publishers and make appointments to hear their songs. Visit them. Have them visit you. So she did, and she told them she wanted to hear more traditional country. And they tried to give her what she wanted.

Bowen is a man who respects his artists' talents and believes in giving them a lot of say in the songs they record and how their records sound. Working with Bowen, Reba found herself more and more responsible for her music, and she took on this responsibility gladly. Over the next few years, she blossomed into song selection, production, publishing, and numerous other related enterprises. Given her strong personality, she eventually would have taken more control over her work even without Bowen. But Bowen's positive attitude probably accelerated the process. About her first album with Bowen, *My Kind of Country*, Cusic quotes her as having said, "I picked every song on the album. There isn't a string on it besides fiddle, and there's no synthesizers."

Bowen had her sitting in on the mixing and mastering processes and encouraged her to make suggestions about instrumentation and arrangement. This album, more than any other album she had ever recorded, reflected the feelings and tastes of Reba.

Reba with Vince Gill.

And when October came around, the Country Music Association voted her Female Vocalist of the Year. From hereon in, Reba's career would belong to Reba.

Now, it's easy to put a feminist slant on this story, and such a spin might be justified. But it must be kept in mind that in the past, country music producers controlled the recording direction of most artists, male and female. Reba was not just a pioneer for women in gaining greater control over her recording career but also for men. Along with Dolly, Waylon, Willie, Kenny Rogers, and Bowen, Reba was instrumental in changing the way all country artists in Nashville do business.

Today it is common for producers and record executives to allow even brand new artists to follow their tastes and instincts in recording material. At one time many artists breezed into town off the road and expected their producers to have selected all the songs for them to record. Today most artists know that they will be expected to be a key part of the song selection process.

But is country music better for the change? Who chooses better music, the artists or their producers? I believe that on the whole the songs you hear in country music today are better than the songs you heard twenty years ago. And whoever is better at picking songs, there is bound to be more diversity in country music when the artists have their say. After all, an artist only has one artist to worry about, while a producer might have more than a dozen artists for whom to find songs.

The years have gone by and Reba is hotter than ever, thanks to more exposure through stunning videos and movie roles. As this is being written, Reba has two albums on Billboard's Top Country Albums chart and both of them are double platinum. She's the only female country artist enjoying that kind of prosperity at this time. And all this is happening after a decade as a top selling, award-winning country artist. How has her career managed to stay at a peak for so long at a time when the pundits are insisting that country music's younger demographics means shorter careers for country artists?

Ed Morris, *Billboard* columnist, sees it this way:

"I think it all has to do with that ability to replenish oneself. . . . The ability to change is everything because Reba McEntire was still wearing rodeo buckles and fringe skirts up into the eighties. And I think when she realized that she had to quit this 'rodeo brat' image, and go to something more cosmopolitan, more embracing, then I think

Reba performs "Respect" at a CMA show.

that's why she was able to [keep her career in high gear]. Reba to me is a wonderful example of a woman who's changed and changed and changed.

"Dolly sort of took a breathing space when she went to Los Angeles and started to become a multimedia star. Reba for the most part except for certain videos has still been essentially a country singer and has not gone too far outside of that, and I think that within that confine we have seen her change . . . and grow. It's not just changing, and it's not changing with the market so much as gaining more confidence in her own right and then reflecting that confidence in what she chooses to sing."

Reba has an advantage over Dolly in that when Dolly decided to go pop, she was feeling the need to reach out for a wider audience. No country star today needs to do that. Country has become so big over the past few years that to become a major country star means to become a major star in American entertainment. Reba was one of the

first country stars of her time to take that path to national renown, and many of the decisions she made were her own. At this time she is country's biggest female recording star.

In 1991 Reba's band, and her tour manager, Jim Hammon, died in a plane crash on Otay Mountain outside of San Diego. Not long thereafter, Reba herself was involved in a severe plane mishap but escaped serious injury. Terribly shaken by these events, she nevertheless continued to work on a new album, ''For My Broken Heart,'' and appear with Kenny Rogers on his continuing series of made for TV movies called *The Gambler*.

As this chapter is written, Reba's career seems headed to even greater heights. She is on the top rung of female country singers and due to stay there. If you walk down Music Square West on Nashville's Music Row you can see a large hole in the ground. This hole belongs to Reba. In an area known for its major changes over the past three years, she has torn down three old houses-turned-office-buildings and is replacing them with a single building that will be the home of her network of Music Enterprises. The rodeo girl is now a business mogul.

6

Michelle Wright

OVER THE YEARS A NUMBER OF CANADIANS HAVE made great contributions to country music. Hank Snow comes to mind, and of course Anne Murray has been a country star for many years. And now there's a new one knocking on the door. She's Michelle Wright, she sells records, she tears up her audiences, and if she can focus in on just the right material, she could become one of the brightest female stars in country music.

Michelle grew up in Merlin, Ontario, which is about forty-five minutes away from Detroit. Her parents were both country performers so perhaps she was more influenced by country music than by the Motown sound she was hearing just across the river.

Her family was riddled with alcoholism, and early on she suffered with the disease herself. In a 1992 CMA Closeup article, she is quoted as saying the following:

"I came from a divorced family. Maybe all of those elements of my childhood just didn't give me the same sort of security that comes from a family with a mother and father. Often the alcoholic says and does things when they're drinking that's embarrassing and shameful. That shame just piles up over the years, and you lose confidence, you lose self-respect. You lose a lot of things. Now everything I do, I am in control of. Whether it is two in the morning or when I get out of bed, I can remember the night before and therefore there is no shame. There is no hiding of something I may have said or done.''

It is one of the prime tenets of alcoholic organizations that an alcoholic is an alcoholic for life and must fight it every single day. Michelle Wright has been winning the fight for the past five years, during which time she has put together a fine beginning for a career in country music.

Michelle is Canada's foremost country star at this time. In recent years she has been a consistent winner of the Female Vocalist of the Year award by the Canadian Country Music Association. *RPM* magazine, Canada's best known music trade magazine, has given her the Big Country Award for top female vocalist in 1989, 1991, and 1992, as well as Artist of the Year in 1991. And in 1993 she won Canada's prestigious Juno Award for Country Female Vocalist of the Year.

In 1992, she began to receive recognition across the border when the Academy of Country Music tapped her as Top New Female Vocalist. Her albums are beginning to sell in the U. S. as well as Canada. She is *this* close to being a major American country star.

She needs a big hit. There are hits and there are hits. ''I think we already had a couple,'' she said during an interview at FanFair '93 in Nashville. '' 'He Would Be Sixteen' and 'Take It Like a Man' were pretty special songs but . . . we haven't been able to have those top fives and number ones consistently.''

For the record, ''Take It Like a Man'' made it to number eight on the U. S. national charts, and it triggered enough sales to prove that there are a bunch of folks out there ready to put down cash to hear her.

''One great thing about 'Take It Like a Man' is it sold probably three hundred thousand [albums] or better, and it really was the song that turned things around for us.''

There have been a number of country artists over the years who were beloved by radio programmers yet who never caught on with record buyers. On the other hand,

Michelle Wright won the Entertainer of the Year in Canada the same year Garth Brooks won in the United States.

some acts, Hank Williams, Jr., and the Kentucky Headhunters come to mind, have sold huge numbers of records without much support by radio. Like them, Michelle's fans are ahead of radio in appreciating her music.

"It's definitely happening that way, it's kind of strange," she agreed. "But that to me is a good indication that the fans like what I'm doing and that really is the bottom line. Certainly you need the radio folks out there and I understand the challenge that they face. There's a lot of great music out there and a lot of artists sending new product in all the time, but at least I'm able to recoup somewhat to my record company, which then encourages them to re-sign me and allow me to keep recording."

At the time of this interview Michelle was in the midst of recording another album, which would be her third on Arista. What she had to say shed a lot of light on the differences between recording an album today and recording an album a decade ago.

"We've got thirteen tracks done, not mixed, and decisions haven't been made yet on those thirteen [which ones will finally make the album]. We're probably gonna go on and do six or seven more, probably gonna cut about twenty songs for this album and then pick the best ten in our opinion."

Not so very long ago, when an artist cut a ten-song album, they went into the studio and recorded ten songs and hoped that they all came off well, because those were the ten songs that were going to be on the album. Today most country artists over-cut—that is, they record more songs than they intend to use on the album. There are at least two reasons for this. When a hit happens in the studio, it's sort of like magic, and given the unpredictability of the recording process, producers feel that cutting a few extra songs increases their chances of capturing the magic on tape. Second, the more songs you record, the better your chances of pulling off ten excellent cuts for a really high-quality album.

There is a third reason for over-cutting, though I don't

*Michelle is joined by songwriter Jill Colucci
and singer Wynonna.*

know how many producers actually think this way. There is a certain kind of song so unusual that it may emerge from the studio as a very special recording or it may turn out so dismal that no one would want to let it out of the tape box. A producer would be much more likely to gamble on one or two of those songs if he or she knew he had other songs to fall back on.

Most artists even today do not record twenty songs to get ten, which indicates just how much time and effort Michelle and her producers are willing to put into her recordings.

"This time around I said, let's make sure that we've got ten undeniable, unquestionable songs that can put my career where it should be now. I've been on the road twelve years, you know, I don't have another five or six years to keep laying down the groundwork here. I feel like we've done that now. It's my record company and my producers' re-

*Michelle helps Buddy Killen takes bids for
her jacket at The Stockyard Easter Seal Concert
and Auction in Nashville.*

sponsibility as well as mine to make a great record on me
this time.''

It turned out that all this recording was in vain. Michelle
now has a new producer, and at the time this is being written they have been recording a new batch of songs.

Is there much of a difference between country music in
Canada and country in the United States?

''I got in trouble once when I answered this question
because I said, well, there is no difference, and in so many
ways I think that there is no difference. There are definite
differences in the way radio works, but as far as the music
is concerned, we do have our artists that have specific
sounds, artists from Newfoundland, artists from Quebec,
artists from the west coast . . . we have those people who
bring a very unique sound to their music.

''From the standpoint of radio, we have something called
CanCon. It's a regulation that requires radio stations to play

30 percent Canadian music. . . . A record, to qualify for CanCon, has to be three parts Canadian, which means the producer, the songwriter, the artist or the studio, the songwriter . . . there has to be three of those four elements of the piece of pie that are covered by a Canadian.''

Why CanCon? American popular culture dominates the world. Our music and movies shape attitudes from South America to Asia. Most Canadians live well within range of American radio and television stations. Imagine what would happen to Canada's distinctive pop culture if they allowed it to be drowned out by Hollywood, Madison Avenue, and Nashville. ''I think that we [Canada] as a country need [CanCon]. Because quite frankly if we didn't [have CanCon] I don't know what would be going on with Canadian artists. There still is not a whole lot going on for Canadian artists.''

Over the years in country music there have been a number of men who were not afraid to express their strong opinions in songs and interviews, men like Johnny Cash, Merle Haggard, Charlie Daniels, David Alan Coe to name but a few. Women have tended to be more laid back about baring their souls concerning controversial issues. Michelle does not come off as a preacher, but she's not afraid to say where she stands.

"You know what's so exciting is that today being a woman is the best time. I think that at one time the women out there were not as independent and confident and strong as they are today and I think they found their fantasy in the men in country music. They would go to the shows and buy the albums and . . . that was their fantasy—you know, hubby's at work and [smiles] he got a big ole beer belly— he's comin' home from work and 'you know we're goin' out to see Kenny Rogers or Randy Travis,' and the women would fantasize. And today I think that the younger women aren't all married with children screamin' around them and housework to be done and they're also very used to Janet Jackson and Madonna and Paula Abdul. They're used to women being very strong and very sensual and very proud of what they are. And so women such as myself and some of the young girls you see coming out [and performing], those women are not threatened by us.

"And therefore they bring their boyfriends to the concerts to see us and they buy our records and their lives are very full and very complete and they don't really need that fantasy as much as maybe [they did] at one time. Does that make sense to you?"

There, in a nutshell, might be the difference between female country performers today and those of yesteryear. The marketplace works in country music. Back in the fifties and sixties and early seventies, Kitty Wells and Tammy Wynette were perceived as the kind of women other women could trust with their husbands. Today's female country artists, like Michelle, and Wynonna, and Pam Tillis and even veterans like Reba, Dolly, and Tanya have a swaggering confident stage presence that might have been daunting to Billy Sherrill's prototypical housewife record buyer of twenty years ago.

The men too have changed, Michelle said.

"One thing I find that's just incredible is the number of men that are at those concerts today. I'm on tour with Alabama and Diamond Rio . . . and these are men [who are attractive to women]. But the place had got a gazillion men in the audience as well that just love and admire those guys. Maybe they're there somewhat to see me as well but I think we're seeing a great deal of diversity in that audience where it's not as female dominated anymore, and I think all of that's very good."

Then, getting back to the women, "My goodness, I mean a woman at one time couldn't sell a gold or a platinum album hardly and I just think that's awful. When we have so much to share and so much good music.

"[We can] be strong and really have an image and an idea and an identity and all of those things that we're allowed to have today. As a female I don't go into a studio and look for songs that I think, oh yeah, women are gonna love this! I sing from a woman's perspective, so the women are maybe gonna relate to it, but that's—I think that's very scary when you're gonna go, okay, well would the women like this? Well what about me, do I like it? I have to like that too."

Here Michelle is talking about the old commercial music question, do I use my ears and my heart or do I use my brain? Sometimes when they are searching for hit songs producers think too much and feel too little. It is possible that many bad decisions are made by recording executives who have heard too many songs in their lives. Their eardrums have grown callouses. It is hard to move them with a song. They say, "Does this song have the elements that make it a hit?" instead of, "Does this song touch me?" After a dozen years on the road, Michelle is telling us that songs still touch her, and that she believes she can communicate that feeling to her audiences.

Michelle comes across as strong, independent, inner-

Michelle's first appearance at the Opry.

directed. So where does she stand on her attitude toward men?

"Well, you see, I am very dependent on my mate. Joel [Kane] is my guy, he's my bass player in my band and I don't know that my life would be as complete without him. I count on his strength. He's a very strong man and I feel more complete with him in my life. It's not because he's a man, it's just because of who he is as a human being.

"I hate man-bashing. Somebody asked me if I was a feminist and I looked up the meaning in the dictionary and that is someone who stands for the rights of women, and I do stand for that, but I certainly don't then not stand for the rights of men as well. I think I really sit [on] the fence, fifty-fifty. I think it's from a more compassionate point of view.

"I've been on the road with men for twelve years, now, of my life, and I've learned to understand men a great deal. We're not all that different. We don't want or need all that many different things. I think we want and need the same things. I think we just have to have compassion and understanding for one another on an equal level. . . . Let a man communicate and let him say what he says.

"I just wrote a song recently called 'Let Me Be Your Rock, Let Me Be The One That You Lean On.' From a woman's point of view saying to a man, you know, it's okay for you to be vulnerable as well."

Michelle Wright has all the elements that go into the making of a star: an expressive, distinctive voice, a charismatic, energetic stage presence, an understanding of what it takes to succeed, a powerful commitment to her career, and the ability to work well with good people to reach her career goals.

But all these things are not necessarily enough. Most great careers explode through the power of what is known as the career song. Billy Ray had his "Achy Breaky Heart." Elvis had his "Heartbreak Hotel." Patsy Cline had her "Walkin' After Midnight." Some of the greatest stars in country music have struggled before the career song came. Perhaps by the time this book is published, Michelle Wright will have had hers. Make no mistake about it though, with or without the song that makes her a big-selling country artist, Michelle is one of the most exciting personalities of the women in country music today.

7

Trisha Yearwood

WYNONNA, REBA, MARY CHAPIN, PAM, DOLLY, Patty, Trisha. They're all selling millions of CD's and tapes, and they're all so well known that even for the casual country fans their last names are not even necessary.

But music runs in cycles, and if there is a tiny dark cloud on the country horizon, it was apparent to me in a conversation I had in the summer of '93 with Nashville music veteran Pat Rolfe. "The one thing that worries me," she said, "is that we haven't really broken any new female country stars since 1991." Broken is music-speak for the emergence of a new star.

Her words rattled around her ASCAP office at the head of Music Square West. We thought about it for a moment. During the period since the arrival of the last big-selling female star, a bunch of men have broken through, names like Clay Walker, Billy Ray Cyrus and John Michael Montgomery. There have been some really good female acts knocking on the door; we knew that sooner or later a new female singer would pop out of nowhere and capture the imagination of the listening public. There's just too much talent out there for it not to happen.

The last female act to battle her way to the top was Trisha Yearwood. In fact, her rise was more like a rocket than a battle. Her debut single, "She's in Love with the

Trisha Yearwood makes her video,
"The Wrong Side of Memphis."

Boy,'' shot to the top of Billboard's country singles chart and stayed there for two weeks, very rare for a brand new artist. Her debut album, ''Trisha Yearwood,'' just missed the number one spot, went platinum, and as this is written, has graced the Billboard Top Country Albums chart for more than two years. Her follow-up album, ''Hearts in Armor,'' also went platinum and has ridden the charts for well over a year.

Trisha Yearwood has quietly become one of country music's greatest female stars.

It is normally a truism that to break into show business you have to go where the action is and hang around and get to know the movers. Somehow you have to get yourself through those locked doors.

In the sixties and seventies that was fairly easy to do in Nashville because, in fact, the doors were not locked. You could walk down Sixteenth or Seventeenth Avenue South until you found a publishing company that didn't look too frightening and then you'd walk in and probably find someone willing to listen to your song. Music publishers were your entree into the record companies, if you could impress them with your talent.

As the business got bigger and more impersonal, publishers and record companies began to avoid strangers off the street and install voicemail, making it much harder to break into the big-time world of country music.

And yet, for the young person with an academic bent and a sense of commitment, there is a legitimate way to get yourself into the music business in Nashville. This is the route that Trisha Yearwood took.

That route is Belmont University, a Baptist-sanctioned school located just a few blocks away from the magnolia-lined avenues of Nashville's Music Row. At Belmont, in addition to other, more ordinary pursuits, you can take courses in music business and management, studio engineering, songwriting, music—most of the areas that are vital to the industry. Equally important, up and down Music Row there are labels, publishers, and other music industry companies that will take interns from Belmont.

Belmont has had its music business school for more than two decades, and the Nashville music industry is loaded with graduates of the university and the intern programs. Many of these graduates have great success stories to tell. Trisha Yearwood is one of them.

Trisha was raised in and around Monticello, Georgia, which is just three counties southeast of Atlanta, by her schoolteacher mom and banker dad. Early on, they moved out of town to a thirty-acre farm. Lisa Gubernick, in her perceptive biography of Trisha titled *Get Hot or Go Home*, describes that farm as "the small-town southern version of the postwar middle-class dream."

Overall that is a good description. For many older rural

*Trisha at the Women in Country Music TV show
rehearsals in 1992.*

southerners, their childhood on a farm was hard and poor.
But quite a few of those who made it into the suburban
middle class longed to return to their uncluttered country
roots. Consequently, many areas of the South are dotted

with hobby farms of ten to fifty acres where merchants, lawyers, salesmen, and bankers can run a few cattle, plant a few acres of soybeans, grow a little orchard, and rewrite their childhood, editing out the bad parts. In fact, many of these merchants and lawyers may be a generation or two removed from the soil, but the farm life still has an attraction.

It's a nice lifestyle, and not a bad way for a child to grow up. Trisha grew up with her older sister, Beth, and according to various accounts, while they were close, Trisha was the more adventurous of the two.

Some of you have probably wondered what it is in a child's life that gives her the confidence to take a gamble like committing herself to being a country star. After all, it's not simply a matter of investing a couple of years and then, after failing, trying something else. It's a matter of getting close, then trying again, year after year, while all the other options you have in life close down on you one by one. Then, if you live in a small town, everybody knows what you tried to do and when you finally give it up, the mean-spirited ones shake their heads at your folly. Who did you think you were that you could make it big coming from a little town like Monticello, Georgia, or Sevier County, Tennessee, or wherever?

In a 1992 *Country America* piece written by Neil Pond, Trisha was quoted as follows: "My parents always encouraged us to do whatever we wanted to do. . . . When I told them I wanted to be a singer, they didn't think I was crazy. . . . I think some people thought, 'What a shame. Trisha could have gone out and done something with her life.' Other people may have felt that way, but my parents never did."

But why did her parents not try and discourage her? Didn't they know the odds against her succeeding? They probably did. Most of us do. But some people live their lives with the confidence that they will succeed at what they attempt, while others live their lives afraid they will fail.

These attitudes can pass from generation to generation as if they were genetic.

During her high school years she trimmed her first name down from Patricia to Trisha. After graduation she attended a nearby junior college for two years, and not long after that, she decided that she was ready to make her commitment. Off she went to Belmont University, which back in 1986 was still Belmont College.

At Belmont Trisha eased into the music business curriculum, and there she showed some genuine wisdom. Through the years, the singers who have had the longest careers have generally been the ones that treated their careers like a business and never stopped learning the business. I have already talked about the essential role Dolly Parton and Reba McEntire came to play in the business side of their careers. At Belmont, at the very least, Trisha learned the importance of the business end.

"I didn't learn all the answers," she told Neil Pond, "but at least I learned what questions I'd eventually need to be asking."

One of Trisha's first business experiences was in the publicity department of MTM Records. Back in the eighties, MTM was one of a small group of independent record labels that did battle with the major record labels on the country charts. MTM, which stood for Mary Tyler Moore, was a California-based publishing and recording company that had a promising beginning, developing such high-profile acts as Holly Dunn, Judy Rodman, and Girls Next Door. Evidently nobody was able to convince A & R head Tommy West that female recording acts were not a profitable way to go in country music.

So presumably Trisha sat in her publicity office helping to churn out the information and promotional hype for MTM's happening female acts. As it turned out, these fine singers didn't sell enough records to make MTM profitable and eventually the label had to close its doors. By that time, Trisha had made something of a name for herself as a demo singer.

So much has been written in recent years about the music business that many readers will know what a demo singer is, but for those of you who don't, here's a good place to stop and explain because demo work was important to Trisha's career.

Over the past four decades, the primary business of Nashville's music row has been songwriting and song publishing. When a song is born, it usually starts out as a fairly ugly baby, because so many songwriters don't sing or play all that well. So publishers take these songs into the studio and they make a recording of it using the best musicians and singers who will work for demo scale. Artists and producers are like the rest of us. If you play them a beautifully produced recording of a pretty good song, you can fool them into cutting it, although many of them will insist they can't be fooled.

Anyway, when music people hear a great voice on a demo, they always ask, "Who's that?" And then they ask, "How do I get a hold of him or her?" Many current country stars began their careers as demo singers. It's definitely an honorable and educational way to pay your dues and earn a living.

Soon she was singing backup on "real" sessions, such as Garth Brooks's "No Fences" album and Kathy Mattea's "Time Passes By" album.

According to Kate Meyers in *Entertainment Weekly*, Garth was so thrilled early on by her singing he promised her that if he made it big, he'd want her working with him. True to his word, when he made it to the top, he took her on tour as the opening act.

Years ago when you wanted to get a record deal you simply made a demo and sent copies around to the various labels. If they liked the way you sang, they might get interested, and then if they liked the way you looked, you might get signed. Those were the days when being a country star meant singing your heart out for about an hour without a spoken word, kind of like what Conway Twitty used to do, or sidling up to the mike and modestly telling

Fans sing along to "She's In Love with the Boy."

the audience something like, "Here's a song that was mighty good to me a little while back."

Country singers hung around a microphone like a deer hangs around a salt block, and the ones who played a guitar used it as a prop either to hide behind or as a signboard, as Ernest Tubb did when, at the end of his show, he would turn his guitar around and display the word, "thanks."

All that changed when the record labels found they could sell their artists through country videos. It changed further when Garth Brooks began to use the stage as his own public gymnasium and started selling albums at nine million a pop.

So now, before a label will sign a country artist, they want to see him or her perform. Thus we have the showcase. When an artist and manager decide to present a showcase, they first decide on the place, which is usually one of half a dozen listening rooms in Nashville with names like the Exit Inn, Twelfth and Porter, 328 Performance Hall, or the Bluebird Cafe. They then decide whom to invite to the showcase. Naturally they want record executives there;

they're the reason the showcase is being held. It is terribly important that the right ones come, and it's not always easy to get them. After all, there are dozens of singers presented every year, and most record executives would really rather think about other things when their office hours are over. Often the showcases are presented around six o'clock so the record people can come by just before they go home. Food and drink, say, barbecue, beans, and beer, might be provided.

Generally members of the working press are invited, both to further brighten the aura of importance of the occasion and to remind the record people in print about the act they saw (or didn't see) that night. Finally, the artist and manager often invite trusted friends to come out and see the show and eat the barbecue. Their job is to get all excited about the performance of the artist in order to convince the label executives that the artist has charisma.

These showcases can be expensive, especially if the artist decides to hire noted backup musicians. In truth, many of these artists have friends among the town's musicians, and so many of them are pleased to show their stuff that it's not hard for a poor artist to dig up half a dozen fine pickers who will do the rehearsals and showcases for little or no money. Still, the food, the invitations, and other incidentals run into cash, but it's an investment most artists will be glad to make in order to get to perform live in front of label executives. Of course, there is the risk that the executives won't come, or if they come, that they won't listen, or if they listen, that they won't love.

The reason for explaining all this, of course, is that Trisha Yearwood and the producer she was working with, a highly regarded music veteran named Garth Fundis, decided to have a showcase. The place was Douglas Corner, the invitees came in droves, including the record executives and functionaries, and Trisha got a record deal from Tony Brown at MCA. Fundis would be her producer, which made sense because he had already proved himself to be one of the best record producers in Nashville.

Trisha and Don Henley at the CMA in 1992.

At the time "She's in Love with the Boy" was climbing the charts, Trisha was touring with Garth Brooks before huge crowds and that exposure helped her become the first female country artist to hit the top of all the major country charts with her first single.

But Trisha Yearwood is a perfectionist, and her career was not at this time perfect. Bob Doyle and Pam Lewis were handling her management. Doyle and Lewis were Garth Brooks's management, and when you have a runaway product like Garth was, everybody assumes that you must be the finest management team in the history of the business.

It never looks quite that way on the inside. Trisha was on the inside. So she left Doyle and Lewis, and at about the same time left her husband, Chris Latham (the two events had nothing directly to do with each other). After a search, she decided on Ken Kragen as her new manager, which was a super catch for her. Kragen had the track record, which included Lionel Ritchie, Kenny Rogers, and

Travis Tritt, he had the L. A. base, always a strong lure for a very ambitious country artist, and he was so successful that he was not the kind of man to get himself involved in a new artist's career unless he was certain that he had, in showbiz lingo, a monster on his hands.

Fortunately for Trisha, Kragen had already been hearing good things about her, and soon the two had a management deal.

As this book is written, her career has soared upward, with the two aforementioned platinum albums, a body slimmed down to near-Hollywood standards, million dollar road tours, and a starring role in Revlon's seven million dollar ad campaign for Wild Heart cologne.

Why has Trisha been so successful in such a short time? Is it the quality of her albums? Her stage abilities? The show business acumen of Ken Kragen? The irresistible momentum created by a great first single? Trisha's tough, driven, business-oriented dedication?

One of the fun things about the music industry is that everybody has an opinion and nobody knows. But there is one thing easy to predict about the future of Trisha Yearwood's career. Because she is a great music fan, as well as a fine singer, she will be, like Dolly and Reba, the moving force in the choice of her song material and her musical direction. Do not expect her to re-create her successes. Her strong vocal talent gives her the freedom to stretch her musical horizons, and like Reba she will do just that.

A fitting ending to this chapter is a quote from an article by Robert Hillburn, celebrated music journalist for the *Los Angeles Times*.

When Trisha was visiting a station on the West Coast, a woman came up to her and handed Trisha a voice tape of her daughter. While Trisha signed autographs, the little girl began to sing one of Trisha's hits.

"I always wanted to be a singer, just like that little girl, [Trisha explained later] but I didn't tell anybody about it because it seemed like something that was impossible, coming from Monticello, Georgia.

Trisha and her celebrated manager, Ken Kragen.

"Everybody knew I was into music, but all that meant in our town was that you either taught music in school or led the church choir, because that's what people who were interested in music did there. Just the idea of moving to Nashville seemed impossible enough, much less becoming a singer there.

"Sometimes I still wonder how I ever did it."

8

Behind the Scenes

OFTEN THE MEDIA OVER-PROMOTES THE BIG STARS IN such a way that the public does not get an opportunity to see how the music business really works. There are even people within the music business who have a very limited idea of how it works.

Although there have been female country stars for many decades, it is only in the last thirty years that women have begun to assert their presence behind the scenes and only in the last ten that they have really broken down the walls in the workplace. A few of the walls are still intact, but we shall see for how long.

The founding fathers of Nashville's country music industry were exactly that. There were no founding mothers, at least none in overt power positions. Then, in the sixties and early seventies, women began to be noticed in positions of authority, notably as executive directors of organizations, like Jo Walker Meador of the Country Music Association and Maggie Cavender of the Nashville Songwriters Association.

But there was one other woman who became one of the mightiest, most important forces on the Nashville Music scene. Her name is Frances Preston, and she was the head of BMI in Nashville.

"What is BMI?" you ask, yawning so hard that you can

barely get the question out. Without BMI and ASCAP there would be no country music business. Period.

The country record business revolves around songs. The hits get played on the radio and television. The songwriters that write the hits, and their publishers, get paid a lot of money when their songs get played on radio and television. In the past record companies have been known to withhold royalties from publishers and songwriters for their own arcane bookkeeping reasons. But BMI, ASCAP, and their little cousin SESAC, never let the hit songwriters down. Year after year they collect fees from the users of music: radio and TV stations, night clubs, etc., and distribute the money to the songwriters and publishers on the basis of surveyed airplay or chart performance.

Back in the 1960s, before the older organization, ASCAP, had established a strong presence in Nashville, BMI was on Music Row, and the local chief was a tough, ambitious, intelligent, and, yes, attractive woman named Frances Preston.

Frances saw her job as much more than a payout office for hit songwriters and publishers. She looked and she listened, and soon she found that there were some very smart and talented people walking around the row without two dimes in their pocket to rub together. Many of the most successful Nashville publishers and songwriters of the sixties and the seventies owed their start to the encouragement of Frances Preston—and the advances she supplied them out of the coffers of BMI.

Why is this important? Because the Nashville music business is built on a foundation of music publishing and songwriting. You can cut great country records in Los Angeles. You can market them out of New York. But if you want hit country songs, Nashville is the place to find them. And it is reasonable to say that Frances Preston has done as much to build the publishing foundation of Nashville as any single individual.

So I guess I'll have to change what I said a page back. Frances Preston, who now heads all of BMI out of her

Frances Preston, a founder of Music Row.

office in New York City, is truly a founding mother of
Music Row.

A number of women have followed Frances's footsteps
and are carving successful careers in the Nashville music
business. They will tell us their stories, where women have

gone and where they're going in country music. They also have some special insights about the female stars and their music.

Pat Rolfe came to Nashville in the mid 1960s and spent many years at the top of her profession, which was the art of songplugging. Today she is director of membership relations for ASCAP, where she uses the skills she developed working with songwriters over the years to keep them happy with ASCAP.

Pat comes from Waverly, Tennessee, a small town about sixty-five miles west of Nashville. Unlike a lot of music business people, Pat was not drawn to the music industry by the glamor or the opportunity to be close to the stars.

"I was studying to be a surgical nurse at Vanderbilt University," she recalled, referring to Nashville's most highly regarded institution of higher learning, "and my roommate worked for a company on Music Row called Hill and Range Songs. Well, I had to be in full scrub on the operating room floor at six o'clock every morning, and my roommate didn't have to go to work until ten, so I was kind of jealous of her. Then one day she decided to get married and moved to Washington, D. C., and Lamar Fike [who was running Hill and Range at the time] called me and asked me if I'd like to take Claudia's place, and I jumped at it.

"So my joke has always been I've gone from sutures to songs.

"Back then there were no female executives on Music Row except Frances Preston and Mary Reeves Davis," she recalled. Frances we've talked about. Mary Reeves Davis is the widow of country music's immortal balladeer, Jim Reeves. For many years after his death she ran his publishing company successfully.

"And back then, everybody was a secretary," Pat continued, meaning that that's what women did on Music Row in the early seventies. "Now there are no secretaries, they're all assistants.

"Basically, it was just a girl Friday job. [The company

staff] was just Lamar and me, and some songwriters. But what's funny is when I took the job he asked me if I could type and take dictation and all that secretarial stuff, and of course I said yes, and I didn't have a clue.

"[So if she had to take dictation] what I would do is sit down with my note pad and write my name over about thirty-five or forty times, and a few key words on what Lamar would want to do in his letter, and then I would go in and type it, very slowly, and then get it back to him, and he would say, 'Is this what I said?' and I would say, 'Yeah, but I had to change it up a little bit to make it correct.' It worked."

So how did she make the jump from dictation and typing to music?

"Well, you know in the music business somebody always has to give you a chance to get out of the secretarial pool or you'll never ever rise above it. There are some people in the music business who I think should have been executives—female executives—many years ago but they still haven't gotten the opportunity to move that one slot up. I was fortunate enough to work for two men in New York named Gene and Julian Aberbach. And Lamar left Hill and Range in 1972 to go on the road full time with Elvis—he was one of Elvis's big friends. So Gene and Julian called me and I went to New York and met with them and they decided that since I knew the catalog and I'd been there six years, they were gonna give me the opportunity to run Hill and Range.

"So I became general professional manager in 1972."

And what were her duties?

"Signed writers and pitched songs, what every publishing company has done from time immemorial up to now."

That's a little too general a description to really give the reader an idea of what happens inside a music publishing company. Publishing executives must not only decide which writers to sign but also must encourage them through the inevitable unproductive periods, decide which songs are worth spending studio budgets on, figure which artists are best for the songs, then decide who in the recording chain is the best person to pitch the song to in order to get the song recorded. It's a tough job with so many pitfalls and so much pressure to get songs cut that the songplugger might be the most underrated and underpaid of all the music business professionals involved in the creation of a hit.

"To the best of my knowledge [with the exception of Mary Reeves Davis] I think I was the only [woman doing that particular job]."

The competition among publishers to get their songs recorded by major artists is furious, and Pat was competing in a virtually all-male world.

"And you didn't meet with the artists," she remembered. "Back in the seventies, you had to meet with the A & R people and the producers. You didn't pitch songs to anybody but Billy Sherrill or Jerry Kennedy or Jerry Bradley or whoever was recording the artist." This meant that even if she was pitching for a female artist, it was a man who was listening to all the songs coming in and deciding which songs the artists would choose from.

"I don't think it was really different [the fact that I was a woman pitching songs]. I had already put six years in on Music Row, and I'm fortunate enough to have grown up with five brothers, which kind of gives me a little bit of an edge in dealing with the opposite sex. By this time I wasn't the new girl on the block anymore, and I think that my writers were good enough and my songs were good enough, and it still always goes back to the songs, where I didn't have, really, any problems.

"I was smart enough to know that I wasn't a musician or a producer, so when Dallas [Fraser] and Doodle [Owens] [two of Nashville's finest hit songwriters of the time] would go into the studio and do a demo session, I would be there for moral support, but I just kept my mouth shut. And then they'd bring the songs in, and I'd decide who to pitch it to, and try to get a song cut."

It's not easy to get a song recorded, and it never has

Garth Brooks, Pat Rolfe, and Sandy Brooks.

been, but success as a songplugger came fairly fast to Pat Rolfe.

"Things were so different back then," she recalled. "When word got out on the streets that Dallas Fraser and Doodle Owens were goin' in to do a five- or a six-song demo, we would have several artists and producers that would come by the actual demo session and ask for the song that was being demoed at the time. So I'm not gonna say that I was an awesome songplugger, I'm saying we had some great writers."

In those days Music Row was a cozy place where everybody knew each other and life was much more relaxed. But basically, songpluggers did about the same things then that they do now.

"You get into a routine like any other job. I'd call [the various record companies] about once a month, see who was goin' in the studio, who was producing, try to get an idea of what they were looking for, such as up-tempo, a ballad, a song like the last song they had out, and then I would get out their last album . . . and I would listen to the album, try to get a feel on what kind of songs they liked, subject matter, anything that would give me a handle on it.

"Back then we would pitch either a little Wollensak quarter-track tape . . . or if we had an emergency pitch I ran over to Music City Recorders and had a dub made. If you had to carry around four or five dubs in one day it could make one arm longer than the other."

Here a little explanation is required. A Wollensak tape recorder was simply a home, reel-to-reel recorder that you could connect up to your sound system if you needed to make a tape copy of one of your songs. The "dub" is an acetate, a metal core disc with a plastic coating that was essentially an instant phonograph record for pitching a song to someone who didn't have a tape machine available for listening.

"I had a book that I kept all my song titles in . . . and we didn't have that many writers, so I would sit and look at all the titles, 'cause you could remember every song and how it sounded, and try to pick out the songs that would fit the project that you were pitchin' for, and then put together a tape. Back then you usually had to take it and deliver it instead of having the people come to your office. Normally you'd do about four songs per tape because you didn't want to wear somebody out.

"I hired Celia Hill (now Celia Froehlig) as my secretary in the seventies and we worked very well as a team, and one day we decided to go up and see Ron Chancey, who was working for ABC [Records], cutting the Oak Ridge Boys. We were sitting in the outer office . . . and all of a sudden through the wall we heard 'Y'all Come Back Saloon.' Well, we looked at our tape, looked at the four songs we had on the tape, and I put it in my pocketbook. We went in and sat down and visited with Chancey and then he said, 'Well, did y'all bring me anything for the Oaks?' and I said, 'Nope! We didn't, because what we heard through the wall would just now beat anything we had on the tape and there's no use wasting your time and mine.' ''

''Y'all Come Back Saloon'' went on to become the Oak Ridge Boys' first country hit, paving the way for one of country's most successful singing groups. Like many successful songpluggers, Pat Rolfe was afraid of destroying her credibility by playing a producer a song that wasn't good enough.

In the music business few things stay the same. ''In 1975,'' Pat said, ''Hill and Range was sold to Chappell Music, so I went over there and became a member of the Chappell Music team, and I stayed there until 1987.''

By that time Chappell was one of the biggest music publishers in the world, but in 1987 Warner Brothers Music was able to gobble up the gigantic Chappell catalog, and it was then that Pat went to work for ASCAP. The Chappell sale was symbolic of the radical change going on in the music business and the government. There had been a time when record companies were afraid to get too much into publishing because the government might take antitrust action against them, but in the eighties major record companies took heart and bought up some of the most successful music publishers in Nashville. Pat said that up until 1986 the music business in Nashville remained simple. Then various American and international groups began buying up the great Nashville music publishers.

''These were such major money deals, with mega-dollars being spent, that a lot of eyes turned south toward Nashville. . . . A lot of people in the big world of business didn't have a clue about how much money country music was bringing in even then. Since then [1986] just about every company that can be purchased has been purchased. . . . When Buddy Killen sold Tree to Sony, that was just about the end of it.

''[The music business] has become a whole lot more corporate. There's been a big commitment to Nashville,'' she said, and began to name all the huge buildings that giant international corporations were putting up around Music Row.

Okay, so the music business in Nashville has changed, but how has the role of women in the music business changed?

"I've been around for so long that I don't consider myself really a woman on Music Row. I'm a membership rep for ASCAP. Women in general made great strides. . . . I don't know if it's happening in corporate Nashville outside of the music industry, but there are more women executives on Music Row than I ever dreamed would happen.

"Back in the sixties when I came on board you wouldn't have your Donna Hilleys [head of Sony/Tree in Nashville], your Connie Bradleys [head of ASCAP in Nashville] . . . Susan Burns is running Famous [a well-known international publishing company], Celia Froehlig is the vice president of EMI Music Publishing in Nashville, Tabatha Eads is running Great Cumberland Music Group, Martha Sharp and Page Levy are A & R directors at Warner Brothers. I think it's wonderful. I think the music business recognizes talent and ability and not gender."

In particular, women seem to have made great strides in the A & R departments of record companies. A & R people look for songs for the artists to record. They also take care of various artist problems, like helping them find the right producer and acting as a go-between with the support people at the record label. A & R people are also the ones who look for new artists to sign on the record label.

Anyway, why have women become so successful in the A & R field? Pat Rolfe believes its because "Women are very good at picking hit songs. I think demographically that women still buy more records out there than males do, so women are picking songs that other women would like to hear on an album whether it's by a male or a female or a group or a duo or duet, whatever you wanna call it. They have an innate feeling for what is a good song for a particular artist, and what would appeal to another woman in the record-buying public."

Lari White and Rodney Crowell.

Her brow furrowed for a moment as she talked about the abilities of women to select songs for female artists to sing.

"There is something I don't understand . . . that we haven't broken a female artist. It'll be three years in the spring since Trisha Yearwood broke out. You sit back and look—there have been no [new hit] female [acts] . . . since Trisha."

Is she worried about the lack of new successful female acts?

"I'm curious about it. It's always been traditionally harder for a female artist to break than a male artist."

Does she feel that any new artists are on the verge of breaking?

"There's a very talented girl on RCA Records named Lari White. I listened to her first album and there was not a bad song on it, the production was great, and she's got world-class vocals. And I have a feeling that Lari will be the next female mega-star to come into Nashville."

For all the progress women have made in the Nashville

music business, they have not really broken through as record producers, nor has one headed a major record label yet. Why not?

"Maybe a woman hasn't taken an artist in and done some sides and pitched it to a label yet," Pat said. What she means, I believe, is that although there are women who want to be producers, none of them has aggressively pursued the usual path of finding an artist she believes could be a hit artist, then recording a session on that artist, and carrying the tape around to the various labels to see if she can get a deal on that artist.

Pat believes that if women would do that, the way male producers have been doing it for years, then female producers would get their share of deals. "Everything is so competitive nowadays," she said, "that I believe if you brought in a smash act, with four absolute killer singles on it, they [the A & R people] wouldn't care if the devil brought it in."

So her advice to would-be female producers is, "Get an act, go in, cut some sides, give it to a label, and see what happens."

But of course the big question is, When is a woman finally going to get to head up a major record label?

"I think that's gonna happen too," Pat declared, confidently. "There's a lady that works for SBK Records in New York named Terry Santisi, and she's right under Koppelman [Charles Koppelman, head of the SBK publishing and recording empire]. That's a gigantic step for a woman in the music business. I understand that she's doing a wonderful job, and I think other label heads, when they're looking to make changes, [will recognize] that Teri has blazed the trail for women in the record business.

"There's still chauvinism anywhere. It's not indigenous to the South. I think because the South has been portrayed in that manner by people who don't know anything about *us* . . . it's a stigma that we've fought. I've fought it ever since I've come to work on Music Row. If you have a southern accent, they automatically drop about forty IQ points from you, and if you're in a meeting with someone who's non-southern, and you use a word that has more than three syllables in it, it takes them awhile to recover.

"I think that in the music business in general [New York, L. A., and Nashville] they seem to feel that the women can do the job just as good as the men. I don't think the women are making the money that the men are; number one, the women aren't running the record labels where the mega-bucks are going down, but I think that is probably the way it is in any other corporation [outside the music business]. There's a term for it—[it's] called the glass ceiling, where women reach a certain position or get to a certain amount of money and they're not going to make as much as their male counterparts. So I don't think that's indigenous to the music business. I think it's indigenous to corporate America."

One of the women Pat mentioned as a power in the Nashville music industry is Martha Sharp, a senior vice president of A & R at Warner Brothers Records. Martha, more than any record executive, is the person responsible for the resurgence of traditional country music that kicked off the current country explosion. She did it by signing Randy Travis.

Like Pat Rolfe, Martha Sharp got into the music business more or less by accident. "My musical training involved a year of piano lessons when I was about eight," she recalled. "After a year the teacher told my mother she was wasting her money and the piano teacher's time, and so I ended up taking ballet instead.

"A number of years back I happened to be working as a secretary/bookkeeper for a man who owned a building on Seventeenth Avenue South, it was called at that time [now Music Square West], and he rented out his downstairs offices to some people in the music business. It just happened to be Bill Lowrey, ABC Records—the great Felton Jarvis [who later produced some of Elvis's sessions] was working at ABC at the time, [also] Pete Drake [one of Nashville's great session musicians] and Painted Desert Music.

"They would come up to pay their rent and pretty soon I struck up friendships with some of them and got invited to my first recording session. I don't remember who the artist was, I don't remember the song, I don't remember the writer, but I thought, this is a wonderful *thing*! I was just fascinated. Here was this writer who had written the song and I was sitting at the table with him, and here was a singer and here was his producer and all these musicians and they all came in to do the very best that they could possibly do and then, in the final analysis it was just up to the general public. They could say, '*Nah!*' or they could make several people very wealthy.

"My musical knowledge was very slim. I had been voted poet laureate of the seventh grade [at a school in Richmond, Virginia, where she grew up], and I still wrote poetry, and liked poetry, and I thought that this would be a wonderful thing to do.

"My job started suffering immensely, because I was spending a lot of time hanging out at recording studios. I went out and bought myself a forty-three-dollar Kay guitar and chord book and decided that I was gonna learn how to write a song. Pretty soon it came to the point where I knew I could not continue the way I was going. I sold my diamond ring from my marriage and quit my job, got the support of my family, and decided that I was gonna be a songwriter.

"I can remember Ray Stevens saying, 'Why did you give up that great job? You must have been makin' four hundred dollars a week!' And I said, 'Well, you know you just do what you gotta do.' And it wasn't long before I started getting songs recorded. And it was maybe three years before I started having hits.

"I think that being a songwriter is just about the best life that there is."

Martha's hits were big pop hits, not teeny country hits in the days when country hits did not do much for a song-writer's fame or fortune. Her first hit was a classic called "Born a Woman," recorded by Sandy Posey and later,

Martha Sharp and Faith Hill.

much later, borrowed by commentator Rush Limbaugh for use as one of the theme updates on his syndicated radio show.

Posey followed that song up with another Martha Sharp hit called "Single Girl." These songs came out in 1966–67. In that same era Bobby Vee had a big hit with still another one of her songs, "Come Back When You Grow Up." With three big pop hits in such a short time, Martha Sharp had fulfilled her dreams only a few years after she had dreamed them.

"After that," she remembered, "all the people who had passed on 'Born a Woman' and 'Come Back When You Grow Up' decided that they wanted every song that I submitted to them to sound like 'Born a Woman' and 'Come Back When You Grow Up.' And they even said so. Write me another 'Born a Woman!' You know, you didn't like 'Born a Woman' when I pitched it to you the first time!"

Martha's lament is a familiar songwriter's lament. The songwriter is not the star of her song. It takes an almost legendary run of hit songwriting to win for a songwriter the sort of respect that just one or two hit records would win for her if she were a recording artist. Even many of the people who make a decent living writing songs in Nashville must put up with the rudeness of music business people who do not know the names of the writers of the songs that are the reason for their jobs.

So Martha's songwriting career had come to a screeching halt. Why?

"It was a lot of things," she said. "I had bought a nice house with a swimming pool and I was having a lot of fun. I don't know. It just was a bad time in my life in terms of trying to be disciplined. The days would go by when I would float around the pool and I would say, 'Well, if it rains tomorrow I'm gonna write a song.' Or 'After I get the house cleaned up I'm gonna write a song.'

"My mind got off on a lot of other things and eventually, of course, the money ran out and I went to work for Larry Butler."

Who is Larry Butler? One of the best record producers

ever to hit Nashville. He is best remembered for bringing back Kenny Rogers with records like "Lucille" and "The Gambler." He also cowrote, with Chips Moman, "Somebody Done Somebody Wrong Song."

It was a comedown to work for Larry Butler not because working for Larry is a comedown but because a writer of three major pop hits in a year's time generally believes she'll never have to work for *anybody* again.

"I worked for Larry at his production company and then I went with Larry to Tree [Publishing Company, Nashville's greatest homegrown publishing empire] and from there to United Artists Records." Martha didn't know it at the time, but she was paving the way for a second career that would bring her greater glory than her short but sparkling songwriting career.

"Finally one day I just had enough. I'd had enough of Nashville and I'd had enough of the music business and I'd had enough of working in an office where I was expected to fix drinks for everyone, clean up the floor when Larry would come in and take his arms and sweep the tapes onto the floor and say 'Take care of these.' I had just had it, you know.

"So I quit my job and sold my house and went to Lake Tahoe and stayed out there for about four months and came back. . . . It was my intention to get out of the music business forever. I went back to school and studied psychology . . . got [my] masters. I had one class to take and I was looking for some summer work and I ended up filling in at Electra Records as Jimmy Bowen's assistant, and I never got away."

Bowen offered her a job that she couldn't refuse as his assistant.

"I didn't consider myself a very good assistant. But it was great fun because I could just go and sit in Bowen's office and just listen when he'd be on the phone talking to people—he claims he taught me everything I knew. He told me early on that he didn't have time to train me, that I just needed to learn on my own, so he allowed me to sit in there and I learned a lot.

"And after about eighteen months he told me he was gonna make me director of A & R. I said, 'Okay.' I was pretty scared but I didn't look back and I've really enjoyed it the whole way. Well, most of it.

"After a couple of years . . . Warner Brothers and Electra merged rosters. The Warner Brothers staff was let go and the Electra staff became the Warner Brothers staff. Very soon after that . . . less than a year, Bowen decided to go to MCA. He had planned to take a few of us with him, and we were what he called his transition team. Some of us just decided that we felt like we needed to stay with Warner Brothers."

They were taking a chance because the new head of Warner Brothers Records in Nashville, Jim Ed Norman, did not have experience running a major record label.

"We felt that given the opportunity, with a team in place, that he could run a record label. The other thing was that Mo Ostin, the chairman of the board at Warner Brothers Records, is my hero."

She also felt that if she went to MCA Records with Bowen, she would not have the authority to sign acts, which is what all A & R directors long to do.

"[At Warner Brothers] I'd wanted to sign Kathy Mattea. He [Bowen] wouldn't let me. . . . He's very adamant about what he wants and how he wants it done . . . and so I decided to stay here [at Warner Brothers] and it's not a decision that I've ever had a minute's regret about."

You might say she got off to a slow start in the new regime at Warner Brothers.

"That was not one of my better periods of time." During discussions with Mo Ostin on what it might take to make her stay on board with the label she let him know "that I did harbor this hope in the back of my mind that I would be the first female [vice president] at a major record label in Nashville, Tennessee. So I was made a VP, and Janice [Azrak, an executive in another department] was made a

VP five minutes later. So I was still the first.''

She suspected that Jim Ed Norman would have preferred that she be a VP of administration so that he could bring his own studio producer type for the A & R job. "But I just wasn't budging." So Jim Ed and Bowen's "team" who had stayed at Warner Brothers had to learn to adjust to each other.

"We had nothing. Bowen had basically left us with a lot of high-dollar contracts on has-been country artists. The people on the streets never thought we could make it. But Jim Ed said, 'We're gonna try some things. We're gonna take some chances.' And that's what we did. He had, and still has, a wonderful capacity for putting his trust in people and letting them do their jobs without looking over their shoulders.

"And that's what he allowed to happen in the A & R department. I don't think he would have signed Randy at that particular time. But he let me do it. I don't think he was quite sold on Dwight Yoakam, but he let Page [Levy] do that. And I think that that was real important to our success.''

Martha's first signing at the label, and one of the most important signings in the history of Music Row, was Randy Travis. At the time he seemed like a real long shot.

"I was *terribly* nervous. I didn't sleep well for months.'' Although it wasn't such a long time between the time she signed him and the time he hit big, it seemed like years to her. "There certainly was the feeling in my mind that if this one didn't work that I was a goner, partly because everybody thought I was crazy when I signed Randy . . . I still didn't feel secure here [as an A & R VP] and being a woman had a lot to do with that.

"I've never really approached anything I've ever done in the music business as 'I'm a woman and it's gonna be tough.' I've just approached it [as] 'Hey, I can do this.' I have confidence in what I do. The woman thing has come from outside me and sometimes the knowledge that the fact that I'm a woman may be causing problems has had to be forced on me when I didn't really want to see that.

"Women have notoriously been 'light' everywhere in this music business. How many women do you see on recording sessions?"

The answer is, very few.

"How many women songwriters? There are not many. More than there used to be. You know there used to be me and Cindy Walker and Marijohn Wilkin and who else?

"How many producers?"

The answer: Wendy Waldman, and almost nobody else.

"Until you have women producers you may not ever have women [label] presidents. And until you have women musicians you may not ever have women producers. At each stage of the development of music there are not very many women, and the funny part is that women are [the ones who go and buy] our music.

"And yet all these men were making the decisions about what to record, what to put out, who to sign, all of these things. It just made perfect sense to me that a woman would have some kind of an edge in knowing what women like."

There are more successful female songwriters on the country scene than ever before. Presumably they are making an impact in the industry, writing the songs that women can identify with. Does Martha feel any impact from them?

"I don't know," she admitted. "I think we need all the women songwriters we can get, there's no doubt about that, but in listening to songs I don't find that I'm more attracted to women writer songs. There are a few women songwriters that have a uniquely female vision. I think Gretchen Peters is just a highly underrated writer, and I think Beth [Nielsen-Chapman] is a wonderful writer. And Pam Tillis has, uniquely, her own kind of vision. But a lot of writers can write for both [men and women]. I never could."

One songwriter who can is one of country music's more successful female songwriters, Susan Longacre.

Susan grew up in Nova Scotia, Canada, and Ithaca, New York, and spent time in Vermont, Boston, Los Angeles,

*Lib Hatcher, Randy Travis, and Martha Sharp
at the CMA in 1986.*

and New York before coming to Nashville to try her hand
in the country music market.

"I had been playing in bands for about fifteen years.
When I was in Los Angeles I got into a bluegrass band.
One night I met a small-time publisher who was married
to Mary Crosby, who's Bing Crosby's daughter. They had
another writer they represented who lived in Arkansas and
he was a turkey farmer. They wanted to publish the first
song I ever wrote. I sang it one night in a club called the
Banjo Cafe.

"They said, 'Come on over and let's talk about some
business,' so I went over [to their office]. They played me
the turkey farmer's stuff and I thought his melodies were
great but his lyrics were awful. They said, 'Why don't you
send him some [of your lyrics]?'

"So we started writing in the mail. I'd send him a lyric, he'd send me music, then I'd redo the music and send it back. We ended up with about six songs which he demoed in his four-track [recording studio] in the barn.

"Then I had a big heartbreak in L. A. and I decided to go to Nashville. He met me at the Greyhound bus station and we went up and down the street [streets of Music Row] and I got signed at the end of the week. Pete Drake's company. Window Music, it was called."

The late Pete Drake was a steel guitar player, one of Nashville's "A" team—an elite group of studio musicians who got most of the calls when an important recording session was coming up. Drake expanded his activities into publishing songs and producing records and had a lot of success, so Window Music was a plum for a brand new kid in town.

"He was producing B. J. Thomas at the time. I was only there a short while because I insisted on writing things that weren't country and they really wanted pretty traditional [songs], so I ended up going to Welk Music."

Welk Music was the publishing arm of Lawrence Welk's music empire. The Nashville division of Welk Music got a running start back in the seventies by purchasing the fabulous publishing company of Bill Hall, one of the two or three best music publishers in the history of Music Row. Hall remained with the company and ran the Nashville office.

"I signed with Bill and then Bill died about six months later," Susan said. "And I was left with nobody who knew who I was and I talked faster than anybody else."

That last statement may have been Susan's way of saying that in those days there was still a culture gap between the southerners in the country music business and those who came down from the north. "I was kind of a fish out of water, you know?" she recalled.

"So I learned how to do it myself and it was really great."

What was she learning to do by herself? Mostly pitch

songs. Many professional songwriters write for publishing companies that have songpluggers like Pat Rolfe, songpluggers whose job is to take the songs they believe in and try to persuade producers and artists to record them. The luckiest songwriters find a songplugger in their company who believes in them and pitches their songs all over town. But in a publishing company of any size there's a tendency for the songpluggers to pitch the music of some writers and ignore the music of others. The songwriters who are being ignored can either sit around and grouse about the unfairness of it all or they can pick up the phone and make their own appointments to pitch songs.

Susan Longacre, being a survivor, chose to pick up the phone. "I just think in general," she said, "that it's a good idea to be able to pitch your own songs."

In recent years she has been writing for Warner/Chappell, one of the largest music publishers in the world.

"I've always had a lot of support from the pitchers [songpluggers] at Warner/Chappell and [have] gotten somewhat spoiled because I don't do as much as I should." During these last few years her songwriting career has really exploded, which she attributes more to the way the industry has changed than to the way her writing has changed.

"I feel like I was writing things that were sort of 'outside,' and country got big enough to contain 'outside.' I really want to write things no one else is writing. I really don't want to write what's out there on the radio."

This attitude contrasts with the way so many Nashville writers work. When they first come to Nashville, most writers are excited about the process of creating a song, but as they go through the inevitable sequences of acceptance and rejection, and they find that they like the word yes better than the word no, then their writing changes.

Soon they find themselves writing songs like the ones they are hearing on the radio. As this book is being written, country music is adjusting to the changes of the past three years. Thanks to line dancing and songs like "Achy Breaky

Heart" and "Boot Scootin' Boogie," the word is out that radio is looking for hot production records that folks can dance to. That makes label executives tell publishers, and publishers tell their songwriters that the time has come to stop writing heart-rending country songs and start writing "feel" songs with rhythmic riffs and hooky phrases.

Susan Longacre is determined not to live from fad to fad. "I want to be the first person to write a race song for country music. Nobody's done that. I want to write about issues that people are just beginning to accept and [that are] just beginning to be allowed on the radio."

Note what she did not say. She did not say, "I want to write songs that radio will *not* want to play." A songwriter who does not write songs that get played on the radio does not write songs that will get recorded. A songwriter who does not get her songs recorded is a songwriter without a voice.

Susan Longacre is a professional songwriter. She wants to be accepted as she is but she does want her songs to be heard. "I think I was probably one of the first people that wrote a song about a woman who didn't think the family was enough and was trying to expand her life." The song was "Is There Life out There?" one of Reba McEntire's biggest and most exciting hits.

She cowrote the song with Rick Giles, but the idea was hers. "I wrote the lyric and Rick Giles did the music on it. Well, we did some of it together. But mostly . . . I originate a lyric and then I get with other people and help them do the music. . . . I find that very satisfying because I can say what I want to say. I have a certain vision that really matters to me. . . . I like the cowriting situations where I can be allowed to say pretty much what I [want to say]. And I'm at that point now where I do that with everything I write."

Songs she has written include "Time Passes By," recorded by Kathy Mattea, "Sooner or later," cut by Eddie Raven, "If You Could Only See Me Now," sung by T. Graham Brown, "Leave Him Out of This," sung by Steve

Wariner, and "Familiar Pain," a solid record for Restless Heart. Note how many of these hits were by male artists. There are so many more male artists than female that a woman songwriter had better write songs that men can record if she expects to stay on the charts.

She also had "Time Has Come," the title song for a Martina McBride album, as well as her first single, "L. A. To the Moon," recorded by Ronnie Milsap, and "Wild Man," recorded by Ricky Van Shelton. Many of these songs were recorded during the 1992–93 period, and this represents a tremendous amount of activity for one writer. At the time this interview was taking place, she was looking forward to Collin Raye's next single, which was her song, titled "That Was a River."

Susan has been in Nashville for about a decade. Has the Nashville music business changed for women during that time?

"I think it's an about face, from what I've seen," she replied. "Maybe it coincides with the fact that I'm not only a woman songwriter but I'm also successful at this point, so it's hard to separate [the two]. But I feel that the respect level has just gone way, way up. People seek out women writers because they have that perspective, and it's well recognized . . . that women buy most of the country records."

That last insight has been recognized by the country music industry for a long time, but, said Susan, "I don't think they acted on that. Now they're actually saying, Let's see what a woman has to say."

Susan recognizes that there are a number of great women writing country hits today.

"Angela Kaset comes to mind. Victoria Shaw, Chapin Hartford, Liz Hengber—she's doing the great Reba songs, she wrote 'For My Broken Heart' and 'It's Your Call,' Stephanie Davis, there's a lot more. I mean, I was the only female writer at Welk. And there were forty-five writers. And when I went over to Warner/Chappell, there were only a couple of women there and [Warner/Chappell] had eighty songwriters. I think the change has accelerated in the last few years.

"I think along with the acceptance of the fact that women know what women want, I think that women songwriters are just being considered equals in general in this town. There are a lot more who are getting cuts on both male and female [artists]. This is really ironic, because when I started out in this town I made a decision that I wanted to write songs that either a man or a woman could sing, and I wasn't gonna write about women's issues because I wanted to make it as an equal, and I actually wrote quite a few songs that were written from a man's perspective.

"I said, if guys can write songs from a woman's perspective, then I'm gonna [write from a man's perspective] do that myself. And I wrote things that *only* a guy could sing. I mean, I try to do 'I'm a Wild Man' at writers night and that's a little strange. . . . It's just been recently that women artists have even done my songs at all. I still, basically, want to write standards, and I don't think standards have any gender. . . . The heart doesn't have any gender, you know?"

What makes for a successful female artist?

"I have a theory about successful female artists these days," she responded. "[They] are very, very aware of their audience and each one has a very specific audience. Lorrie Morgan has a particular kind of woman [in mind] that is like her and [can] understand her toughness, her attitude towards men. Reba has another particular kind of audience. And I think the women who are really successful have a knowledge of that and then feed into that. There are other women who I think should be bigger, Kathy [Mattea] for example, who have not quite focused on Who is my audience?

"And I think they would do well to be doing some more songs that [relate to] . . . specific things in women's lives."

Are the female artists who control their own destinies,

like Reba and Dolly, more likely to have their finger on the pulse of their audience?

"I don't necessarily agree with that. Kathy, for example, very clearly knows what she likes, and I think she's done some of the most incredible songs that have been done, but I think there's some pulse missing between what she likes and what all the women out there like. I don't want to pick on her 'cause I love her stuff a lot. Kathy herself has a bigger view of the world than some people do and she doesn't have 'an attitude.' She's very involved in her material. It may be more an astuteness [that comes] from experience. Reba knows what her audience wants and she gives it to them."

Who are the audiences that some of these artists are connecting with?

"I think [Lorrie] has focused on women who have had some anger at men, who have had bad experiences with men, whose lives are not easy.... They work hard, they maybe don't get paid as much as they should. It's a whole attitude.... She really does this very well and arouses emotions in her listeners. She knows she's doing that and I think that's really good.... That's one reason why she sells a lot of records and has big hits.

"And Reba talks about women who have children, maybe perhaps an older demographic [than Lorrie]. I mean Reba's demographic is huge because look at her sales. She has a tendency to talk about women who are in relationships that are either breaking up or there are children involved—a lot about families and homes.

"I don't think Mary [Chapin Carpenter] has any limitations at all. I think she's just really on the pulse of women's lives in a big way. Even some of the songs that have never been singles like the one about the shirt. She talks about this guy's shirt. It's still in her closet and all the memories it evokes and how she likes to wear it sometimes and how the whole history of their relationship is in the shirt.

"[Tanya Tucker does] real sensual songs for the most

part. I think part of [her success] is her terrific grooves. Sometimes it's country but it's got a lot of rhythm in it.

"Suzy Bogguss . . . is dealing with the same kinds of women that Reba is. That song about the girl going off to school . . . touched so many people's hearts because no one had ever talked about that before. It was just waiting to happen."

What about K. T. Oslin?

"Boy, she was right on it! I mean as far as women's lives. My God. Nailed, you know? I don't know why she's not still [hitting big] except there may be a move toward traditional and she's not [a] traditional [artist]. . . . She had the spotlight right on her audience. In a sense *she* was what she was singing about.

"And Wynnona has everybody from six-year-old girls to sixty-year-old girls and I don't know if she's focused on her audience so much as that she *is* her audience.

"She has such an incredible voice and does such a wide range of genres really. She does all that rock stuff; I don't know if you've heard her latest album, but it's not country, not really, you know? And so she's bringing all those young teenagers in. They love Wynnona. She can do anything! She's the one female on the radio that can do any kind of song and still go to the top."

Why is it that no modern female act has come forward, like Randy Travis or Mark Chesnutt or Alan Jackson, with a committed traditional country outlook?

She thought carefully before she answered. "I think it partly has to do with the material, that they're [women are] stretching as far as subject matter goes, as far as everything, melodies go, rhythms go. I think they have to stretch to be able to talk about everything that's going on in women's lives. From a writer's perspective, I think there are certain songs that you can't do country, unless Vince Gill is singing them. There are melodies and chord changes that automatically would kind of be outside of country."

A bit of explanation might be useful here. The term "country" means at least two different things. From an industry point of view country can either mean that music, country, pop, rock, or whatever, can be played on country radio stations or can be sold through the country divisions of record companies, or it can mean that part of country music that has fiddles and a steel guitar, as in "that last Garth Brooks record was a real country record, a classic honky tonk singalong," meaning it was more like "Friends in Low Places," than "The Dance," which was a universal romantic ballad.

There are women out there, like Reba, or Patty Loveless, for example, who could fit the mold of the traditional country singer, but they do not choose to.

"I think the quality of the voice has something to do with it," Susan suggested. "Not that you can't be a great singer and sing country, I don't buy that at all, 'cause there are a lot of them that are.

"But I guess if it was me, I wouldn't want any limitations. I certainly would be aware of some of the rules, but then I might try to break them, you know? That's what I've always been doing anyway, and I have a feeling that some of the new female artists feel the same way. It would be hard to imagine 'Wind Beneath My Wings' being done as a three-quarter country waltz. The song itself has a life that has to be honored, in my view, and some of the songs these women are picking, they're bigger than any format.

"I would hazard a guess that people like Trisha and Wynnona and Reba get such joy from the act of singing that they wouldn't want limitations on what they sing. And especially Reba, who thinks about her audience, she goes for the song. She says this is what I want to talk about, I want to sing about this subject, and the limitations on the song—I don't think that that matters to her. And she can get away with it. I mean she has some of the biggest sales in country.

"But here's an interesting thought. She has a country voice. You can't take the Oklahoma out of Reba. And that may be one reason why she hasn't crossed over, whatever that is."

Hit song writer Susan Longacre with SESAC executive
Diane Petty.

Cross over. There is a term that used to be magic in country music. Years ago the ultimate goal of an ambitious Nashville label executive was to try to sign country artists who could "cross over"—that is, go from being purely a country artist to one who sells to pop fans as well. Pop airplay and sales meant that instead of a hundred thousand albums, an artist could sell five hundred thousand or even a million, and they could command much higher concert fees.

Charlie Rich crossed over. Willie Nelson crossed over. Dolly Parton—well, she was a little different. She took dead aim at the pop market and her aim was true.

But today, why cross over toward pop when so many fans seem to be crossing over toward country in search of music with melodies and lyrics? Reba McEntire sells better than two million pieces every time she puts out an album. So she can do the music she wants to do for her audiences and the fans will come.

Does Susan target her songs for different markets? Does she wake up in the morning and say, "Today I'm gonna write a pop song"?

"The song itself defines what it's going to be," she said. "The lyrics particularly define what it's going to be and I . . . like to try to write music that can be any genre."

A little aside about genres in songwriting. A decade or more ago successful country songwriters used to fly out to Los Angeles to cowrite with pop songwriters, hoping to get those prestigious and elusive pop cuts. Today the traffic goes both ways. Successful country songwriters still seek out successful pop songwriters in search of pop connections, but now with the country explosion there are plenty of major pop writers flying into Nashville hoping to cowrite with songwriters who will lead them into the magic world of Garth Brooks and Reba McEntire.

"If I'm writing with somebody who produces [a major artist]," Susan said, "then I'd be stupid not to at least try and write one thing that she might be able to do, and a lot of people from L. A. write with me because they wanna get into the country thing. And I write with them because I like all kinds of music and I'd love to get some pop cuts, even if they're not easy to come by these days.''

Successful songwriters have a good opportunity to observe the changes in the music business. They hang in there year after year and watch people come and go in the record and publishing businesses and are very sensitive to the effects of changes in personnel and the way they do business.

Susan has noted great changes in the role of women on Music Row. "I think some of the best people in A & R are female. I think there are some really good women in publishing now . . . there were hardly any . . . when I first came to town. All three of the performance rights organizations now have very powerful women in them.''

Earlier I mentioned Frances Preston, national head of BMI, who was so important in building the music publishing industry in Nashville. BMI, by the way, stands for Broadcast Music, Incorporated, and is one of the two other performing rights organization in the country. The largest and oldest is ASCAP. The head of ASCAP in Nashville is Connie Bradley, a highly respected veteran of the Nashville music industry.

Diane Petty, another highly respected veteran of the Nashville publishing industry, is a key executive with SESAC, which is the smallest and second oldest of America's performing rights organizations.

"I think they [women] are everywhere [in the music business] and I think it's great.''

Susan noted, as Martha Sharp did, that the one area in which women are not strong is in producing. "And mark my words, I'm gonna get into that!''

Why aren't there more female producers?

"I don't have any clue why not except that people like me and some other people in this town haven't jumped into it.'' Note how similar her answer was to Martha Sharp's. Record producing is a natural outlet for creative people who love the sounds of music. One would think that by now women would have made some inroads into the studio.

"I think it's just a matter of time before a woman finds just the right act to produce," she said. "Obviously it starts with the act, and the field is very crowded right now. You have to have something absolutely undeniable in order to break through that.

"But when I find that, I'm gonna put my hat in the ring definitely. I mean I've been producing my own demos for years."

Here you might ask, does producing demos prepare a songwriter to produce records? The answer is, certainly. Today's studio demos are elaborate; they are meant to sound a lot like records, only they have to be done more quickly and efficiently. But all the processes are the same: selecting the songs, assembling the musicians, deciding how to produce the song, swapping ideas with the musicians on the arrangement and the engineer on the mix, getting the best vocals out of the singers. One of the hottest producers in Nashville today is Don Cook, and Don learned to produce records during many years of producing his own demos in the Tree studio. So the barrier to a writer like Susan is not her studio experience, it's the determination to find a great voice, male or female, and then just do it.

One of these days, Susan Longacre will do it. But, she observed, producing records is not what it used to be.

"I think," she said, "it's a shame that producers don't have more power now. They used to. Producers used to have *the* major power to decide what songs [to record and release] with the artists, and they [record executives] just let them do their thing—that's not true anymore.

"There's way more people involved in the decisions. People who have to protect their jobs, you know, within the label, A & R, promotions, all the people who are astute and running labels are making decisions about the songs and well they should."

Now wait a minute Susan. First you say it's a shame that producers have lost their power to make decisions and then you say all those other functionaries should have a voice in those decisions. Which is it?

"Well I think there are certain people in this town who can. Let's put it that way.

"I'd much rather see the label that has one person at the top who really knows what they're doing and says this is how it's going to be. There's . . . [too] much committee [decision-making] going on now. But there are certain heads of labels in town who are well qualified to be involved in the decision-making process. And their labels are doing very well.

"There are more . . . layers that you as a songwriter . . . have to get through to get to the artist. I mean it's even more difficult for a songwriter like me or anybody to get to the artists now because they are working harder than ever and they're gone more than ever [on the road performing] and some of them are writing with songwriters now."

Let's sort this all out because in these few short paragraphs Susan has sketched out an important part of the music industry that TV and print journalists seldom talk about—either because they don't really know about it or because they don't think the public will be interested.

Actually she has talked about two things—how people decide which songs get recorded and how people decide which songs become singles, those songs that will be promoted for radio airplay.

First let's talk about who decides how songs get recorded. It used to be, as Susan pointed out, that songwriters or publishers pitched songs to the producer. The producer decided which songs he liked for his artist, then he'd play the songs for the artist. If the artist was new, the producer would tell the artist which songs to record. If the artist was established, producer and artist would confer and agree on songs.

Nashville was a smaller town then. There weren't as many songs being pitched. Today there is a layer of A & R people who screen songs for producers and artists. A & R people generally have no power to say "yes" on a song because no matter how much they like the song, the producer and artist can turn it down. A & R people do have the power to say "no," however. If they say no, then the artist and producer will never get a chance to hear the song. Naturally, veteran songwriters and publishers like to go around the A & R people if they can because that eliminates one more possible "no" from the process.

To make things worse, some A & R people will hire assistants to screen songs for them, especially when the tapes come from songwriters who are not hot at the time. Believe it or not these screeners are sometimes young people just out of college with a three-month summer stint as an intern. So you have the spectacle of a veteran hit songwriter getting his songs heard and turned down by kids who don't even like country music and who would not be likely to recognize a hit country song.

Regarding the second point—everybody in a record company is an expert on a hit song and likes to register his or her opinion. Special experts are the promotion people, who call up the radio stations every day and try to get them to play their records. In fact, their job depends on getting radio to play their records, so when they are present at product meetings, promotion people listen to a song from the point of view of, Can I get program directors at major market radio stations to play this record? To many record promoters a song is a hit if it gets to the top of the charts, even if it does not stimulate album sales.

That's a very limited point of view. Throughout much of the seventies and early eighties the country recording industry was plagued by records that zoomed to the top of the singles charts while the artist was selling twenty or thirty thousand albums. Then Hank Williams, Jr., came along, and later the Kentucky Headhunters, and it didn't matter when their singles did not crack top five because their albums sold like Toyotas anyway.

Many songwriters are not very well informed about the inner workings of record labels. Susan Longacre is. She'd probably make a great record executive. In recent years several labels, notably Arista and RCA, have tapped songwriters to head their country divisions. Perhaps someday a woman will make it to the presidential suite out of the ranks of songwriters.

—Note: Even as this book is being written, MCA has announced the selection of Shelia Shipley to head their new Decca division. She is not a songwriter, but she is the first woman in Nashville ever to head a major record division.

9

Mary Chapin Carpenter

COUNTRY MUSIC HAS FOR AT LEAST SIX DECADES taken its influences from wherever it could find them. But mostly it is the music of poor, white, rural, and small-town southern folk.

And even today, most country stars come from small towns and farms, mostly from the South, or from Texas, which may be considered part south, part west. The values that define country music are still primarily southern and blue collar.

But popular music categories are like roadhouses on the main highway. You never know who'll turn up in them, or why. Remember back in the fifties when mature black entertainers like Big Joe Turner, Fats Domino, and Dinah Washington suddenly found themselves idolized by millions of middle-class white teenagers?

As country music expands far beyond its earlier boundaries, it takes in singers that a few years back would never have belonged. Take Mary Chapin Carpenter, Grammy award winner for her song, "Down at the Twist and Shout" from the 1990 album, "Shooting Straight in the Dark," which went gold, and whose "Come on Come on" album is solid platinum-plus and still close to top ten after a year on the charts.

Her background is about as country as Ed Koch (New

York's former mayor). She grew up in Princeton, New Jersey, where many people knew Albert Einstein personally but never heard of Hank Williams. Her family moved to Japan, where her father was publishing director for the Asian edition of *Life* magazine.

She graduated from Brown University, one of the eight Ivy League schools. Why, then, does Mary Chapin Carpenter fit into country, and why oh why is she selling so many CD's and cassettes?

Vocally she fits into the smooth, folk category, the path that was blazed by Anne Murray and Emmylou Harris, so country fans recognize her as country. Her production (with John Jennings) is heavy on acoustic, solidly rhythmic, and very pleasing to the ears of today's country fans.

But it's the songs that set her apart. Of the twelve songs on her "Come on Come on" CD, two were "outside" songs—the hit, "Passionate Kisses," by Lucinda Williams, and Mark Knopfler's "The Bug," one of those great songs that sticks in your mind forever if you've heard it once. Four were written by Mary Chapin with super-songwriter Don Schlitz, including the hit, "I Feel Lucky." And she wrote six of them by herself.

And what wonderful songs they are, full of tasty, surprising melodies and lyrics that grab you, not with their cleverness but with their emotion and understanding. A great example is "Only a Dream," a song that will touch anyone who has had a brother or a sister they cared about, and she does it without creating a maudlin or melodramatic moment.

Billboard magazine's Ed Morris had this to say about her. "Mary Chapin Carpenter is a surprise. I wake each day wondering how it happened and still don't know how it happened. Because she is the introspective and intellectual sort. I guess how it happened if you want to go on a crass commercial basis was 'Down at the Twist and Shout'; here was a woman known for her cerebral lyrics and her plaintive delivery and all that, and then all of a sudden she does this wild Cajun song and brings in Beausoleil to back

*Mary Chapin Carpenter at the
CMA 35th Anniversary Special.*

her up and then at the CMA Awards she does songs that
show how intellectually animated she is—and I think that's
how . . . but I'm still surprised because there's a lot of depth
in Mary Chapin Carpenter, and there is none of this good
ole girl—you know, I grew up in the country and I wore
gingham aprons and all that—there's none of that with her
and never has been. I've never seen her at all pander to
popularity.

"And still, now she's a platinum artist. She's a surprise
to me."

Ed Morris is suggesting here that female artists in the
past have had to flash their credentials as card-carrying
country girls in order be successful. He almost seems to be
saying that "Down at the Twist and Shout" was meant

to do exactly that, but he doesn't. His admiration for her is obvious, and Ed Morris does not go looking for famous people to admire.

Her biggest challenge is, can she sustain the magnificent quality of her songs? We have seen other artists in country and other fields break through with a fantastic album or two or three, only to fall when the songs gave out. It's hard to live up to the standards of the material on the ''Come on Come on'' album. But I would not bet against her, not on my luckiest day.

There are artists who are successful, but who are never able to garner consistently positive reviews. Other artists thrill reviewers into writing long hymns of praise. Then there are artists like Mary Chapin Carpenter who stir the imaginations of reviewers, wake them up, and make them articulate. I'd like to give you some examples of the things they write about her and the music she makes. Keep in mind, of course, that many of these reviewers did not start out as country fans and are happy to find a country artist to whom they can relate.

Richard Corliss had this to say about Mary Chapin in his review published in *Time* magazine of August 24, 1992:

''With her fourth album, Come On Come On, she displays a fully matured talent, her sure alto caressing a wild variety of musical setting (rock, blues, art song) for her lyrics. Carpenter's literary allusions have run from Eudora Welty to old Geritol commercials, but the usual subject of her songs is love—old love, careless love. So what else is new? The range of feelings she mines. At its best, love is hard work, like a decent blue-collar job ('Everything We Got, We Got the Hard Way'). At its worst, it's the rest of our lives.''

And Steve Hochman in the *Los Angeles Times*, following a performance at the Wiltern Theatre, wrote:

''With her Ivy League roots and I-can-have-it-all stance, Mary Chapin Carpenter is to traditional country music

Mary Chapin sings "Down at the Twist and Shout"
with Beausoleil.

women what Hillary Clinton is to traditional political
wives.''

The seeds of Mary Chapin's musical career were sewn
when as a young child she first picked up a guitar that her
mother had bought back in the early sixties—the heyday
of folk singing. Like many successful executives today, her
father relocated several times in the course of his career. In
1974 he moved his family to Washington, D.C. There
Mary Chapin found the same exciting music scene that so
stimulated Emmylou Harris in her formative years.

There are a number of such scenes that have popped up
around the country over the years, notably in New York's
Greenwich Village and Chicago's Old Town. Clubs spring
up that feature a small stage with an acoustic guitar player
singing sincere songs, sometimes classic, sometimes self-
written, often strong on crafted, meaningful lyrics. Would-
be performers might go to one of these places night after
night, sizing up the talent and getting up the nerve to get
up on an ''open mike'' night and sing a few songs.

Clubs like these often develop their own local stars, and the goal of the open mike hopefuls is seldom more than to become a house singer who actually gets paid to perform in front of audiences.

In 1976 Mary Chapin enrolled at Brown University, which means she must have been an excellent high school student and rolled up some good scores on the standardized aptitude tests. The summer after her freshman year she found herself doing the open mike sets at the clubs. She even had the guts to ask the host of one for a job, and he saw she had the talent, so she spent her summers as a working folkie.

The Washington music scene was so strong that they even had their own awards, known as Wammies. In 1986 she won her first Wammies. By this time she had been a regular on the Washington music scene for nearly a decade, singing a wide variety of songs from blues and selected pop standards to contemporary folk country classics and gradually injecting her own material. Did she have a career plan during her coffeehouse days? Did she want to be a platinum selling star? Or was she just evolving?

The year 1986 was when she and her accompanist, John Jennings, recorded some songs in his studio. The idea was to manufacture a cassette album and sell copies to her fans wherever she played.

During this time she also met Tom Carrico, who was to become her manager. He shopped the tape to various labels and the tracks she recorded in Jennings' studio became her first album for Columbia, "Hometown Girl."

In 1989 she came out with her second album, "State of the Heart." She had some solid airplay records off this one, but it was her next album, "Shooting Straight in the Dark," that established her at her record label with gold sales status.

So where is Mary Chapin Carpenter going from here? And why is she called country anyway? I'll answer the second question first by quoting a lead from Richard Corliss in his August 24, 1992, *Time* review. What he says is so accurate and concise that in some form it ought to turn up in a music history book. "COUNTRY MUSIC, IN CASE YOU CITY folk haven't noticed," he began, "is where pop music went to live. When rock 'n roll settled into the bustling ghettos of white metal and black funk, country claimed the ears of the pop-music homeless—those who like songs to mix catchy melodies with prickly home truths. By reaching people raised on '60s folk music and Beatles rock, country has become suburbanized. It's as much at home in malls and vans as it used to be in grange halls and pickups."

Corliss is only telling the suburban half of the story, of course. The present country explosion began nearly a decade ago when huge numbers of folks began to snap up the records of Randy Travis and George Strait, records so ach-

Mary Chapin receives the CMA Female Vocalist of the Year Award.

ingly traditional in their sound that millions of people who had lost faith in country music returned to it with their arms, hearts, and pocketbooks wide open.

The recent suburbanization of country, which received its greatest push from Garth Brooks, has threatened to overwhelm the traditional sounds because so many record executives and radio programmers are suburbanites. I believe that country's musical roots are so strong and so valid that they will continue to exist side by side with suburban country. Eventually, perhaps, radio and the record industry will figure out a way to re-create the pop music industry in such a way that country no longer is the only place left that will take in the pop-music homeless.

If and when this happens, country will finally have its home to itself. This is a most exciting time in country music, because even as it takes in the pop-music homeless, it educates them, broadens their minds, and woos them away from the media bigotry that for so long has made mean-spirited sport with southern and rural speech, customs, and mores without ever learning what that culture is really about. Mary Chapin Carpenter's music is playing a key role in this process.

10

Patty Loveless

THERE ARE A NUMBER OF FEMALE ARTISTS WHO COULD carry the torch of the traditional country singer. One of them is Patty Loveless. Of the successful ones, she probably comes the closest.

Billboard magazine pundit Edward Morris presented the following viewpoint of Patty:

"Patty Loveless has a very good traditional style and she breaks my heart when I hear her sing but . . . I don't find a central point of view emerging from her work. I think that's probably because she sings other people's songs rather than either writing her own songs or insisting on a certain standard or . . . certain *points* of view; I would hate to think that anyone became doctrinaire in their music in that sense."

Patty Loveless is very special in the country music industry because she started so young, long before Nashville's Music Row was bought up one piece at a time by Californians, New Yorkers, the Japanese and other foreigners. Like *The Natural* she flashed faintly across the horizon then seemed to vanish only to appear many years later as a full-fledged star.

She was born in Pikeville, Kentucky, coal country. Black lung claimed her daddy when she was still very young. One of eight children she was quiet and dreamy. She says about

Patty Loveless on tour with Hank, Jr.

her beginnings, "I always loved music, but I was so shy that when my mother would ask me to sing for company, I'd go out into the kitchen and sing 'How Far is Heaven' real loud, so they could hear me, but I wouldn't have to look at them."

Patty remembered her professional debut in an interview with journalist Vernell Hackett. "I was something like twelve years old and, [the] first time I got paid five dollars . . . it was a little small jamboree, maybe it seated fifty or sixty people [in] foldout chairs in a little old small building. And they had a little stage set up and the whole little country show bit and everything. That was the first five bucks I ever made and it was in Louisville, Kentucky."

She may have started making money singing at twelve, but she was learning the craft long before that. "Mother always had me singin' from the time I was four and on. But my sister Dotty, she's married now, and has kids, and I guess that's the reason she let go of it 'cause, that'll keep you busy, itself. She used to sing and to me she sounded more like Patsy Cline, more than anybody I ever [heard] in my life.

"And to this day . . . I wish that she had continued . . . I saw her play in Fort Knox and she got up in front of those guys, I remember what she had on was a brown suit, this beautiful dark-headed girl who gets up and sings and she's something like twenty, and the guys just go crazy, she starts singin' 'Walkin' after Midnight' and I thought, that's one I wanna do.

"I never thought that I'd be standin' on a stage like Dotty was."

You can almost see the shy girl looking up to her sister, the older one, more experienced and gutsy and talented, and wishing she could be like her.

When you're that shy and you want to sing, it helps to have someone in the family who believes in you enough to give you a push. In Patty's case the believer was her brother Roger. When she was fourteen he would drive her down to Nashville and they would try to figure out how to "get in."

Now that's not an easy thing to do. Every year hundreds of people, many with talent, hang around Music Row, the Opry, and various clubs around town trying to meet people and find a way into the music business. Back in 1971 it was easier than it is now. Patty Ramey, as she was called then, found an admirer in Porter Wagoner, who introduced her to Dolly, who became her hero forever after, even taking her into the ladies' room at the Ryman Auditorium and showing her how a real star puts on makeup in between shows.

"I used to sit around and watch the *Wilburn Brothers* show and the *Ernest Tubb* show when I was a kid," she recalled in her interview with Vernell. "Then the *Porter Wagoner* show came along and Dolly Parton just caught

my eye, you know, here's a girl that come out here and sang what she wrote about, her family and her love life . . . she just kinda put herself into stories. She was a great storyteller, I thought, and it just got me interested in writing. When I went to Nashville, the very first person I meet is Porter Wagoner, so he introduces me to Dolly, and that was a teenage girl's dream because I love that lady. I think she's wonderful. . . . She's meant a lot to me and I think she's meant a lot to my career too.''

In those days among the movers and shakers of the country music industry were a singing duo known as the Wilburn Brothers. Doyle and Teddy Wilburn were members of Owen Bradley's Decca Records roster, and they had one of the more popular nationwide syndicated country television shows. They were also Loretta Lynn's mentors, her management, and publishers.

So Patty must have thought she was ready to lick the world when at the age of fourteen she was signed as a writer to the Wilburns's publishing company, Surefire Music.

The streets of Music Row are still mostly remodeled residences. Most of those old houses at one time or another housed a publishing company or two and every one of those publishing companies at one time or another signed a songwriter who was new in town and was certain that a publishing contract was proof of their having arrived.

Patty hadn't arrived yet, although she did get to appear on the *Wilburn Brothers* show one time. Before too long she left for North Carolina with the Wilburns's drummer. They were married, but did not live happily ever after.

''[I got] kinda trapped into having to put food on the table and [perform in] club acts and other things of rock and roll material, and I'm not really sorry that I did this because sometimes, even though my love was for the music I was raised on, I had brothers and sisters that loved the old fifties rock and roll, and Elvis, of course, you know wasn't really what you'd call 'dirt country.' When I started gettin' into this it taught me how to take my voice in many places that I'd never thought about goin'. It taught me about where I could go with it and showed me some strong points there, stronger points than I thought I had.

"There were some times I'd mix [in my sets] like a Dolly Parton, 'I Will Always Love You.' I'd do a lot of Linda Ronstadt . . . I thought that was pretty close to country . . . and they loved it, they ate it up.

"But then it came to a time that people like Pat Benatar, people like that were comin' along, and groups like Journey, I mean, I was doin' all kinds of songs, even their album cuts, and it kind of steered me away from a little bit more of the hard-core traditional country. But you know, you have a love for it and it's always there. I was basically raised on bluegrass. My father listened to it all the time—Ralph Stanley, Bill Monroe, all those men out of Kentucky and Virginia. As a child, I think when you're raised on things you remember it, it just doesn't leave."

Some readers might ask what a country singer was doing singing all that pop music. Like most of today's country singers, Patty did not limit her voice, or her ears, to country. And ultimately, when you sing in clubs your job is to deliver the music the customers want to hear.

By 1986, Patty had finished her career as a club singer. She returned to Nashville with her ex-husband's last name, got a deal with MCA Records, and by 1988 had her first gold album, "Honky Tonk Angel."

Over the next few years, she won numerous awards, had plenty of hit singles, and came closest of all the female acts to being considered "the real country singing star."

But MCA Records also had Reba, Wynonna, and Trisha, all platinum plus artists, which may have determined her shift to the Epic label, a label that is part of the Sony Music family. Like most successful country artists, Patty was under a heavy touring schedule, and during the latter half of 1992 she noticed that she was having problems with her voice. As Alanna Nash explains it in her article that appeared in *TV Guide*, "Initially she attributed her fatigue on-stage to the emotional stress of leaving the people who

Patty at the Opry.

launched her career and the demands of touring. Then she began having pitch and control problems. When the doctor recommended that she take some time off from touring, Loveless, who was booked for the entire summer, said no.

"But as she continued performing, a blood vessel started leaking and her throat problems grew worse."

Things came to a head one night during an onstage performance with Vince Gill, and in October, when she next saw her doctor, the doctor put his foot down on her touring schedule.

Throat surgery is frightening, especially to a singer, but her first album on Epic which, according to Nash, included a number of vocal tracks re-recorded after surgery, launched a big number one single, "Blame It on Your

Patty at the induction into the Grand Ole Opry.

Heart,'' and as this is being written it looks like Patty's career is once again moving forward.

The image makers have billed her as a traditional country artist. For example, marking the debut of Patty's "Only What I Feel" album, then Sony Nashville President Roy Wunsch, who is one of Nashville's premier industry veterans said, "This project validates Patty as the preeminent hard country female vocalist out there and *more*."

Her label bio echoes the same theme:

"When a new wave of traditionalism swept country music, her brother was back pitching, and it wasn't long before Patty had a record deal.

"Since then Patty has stood for the integrity of hard country music. As she says, 'You're gonna hear that old bluegrass style, those blues licks when I sing. It's who I am—and I can't leave that behind. What we sang growing up was more old mountain style music, white man's blues, and that'll always be in there!' ''

I think what bothers some observers is that some of her big radio hits, notably "Timber, I'm Falling in Love," and "Blame It on Your Heart," are not hard-core mountain music, but a little more like radio candy, the country equivalent of the old rockin' pop music like early Beatles or Dave Clark 5. But it's not at all uncommon for artists to release certain records as singles to please radio and their drive-time listeners, while the overall tone of the album is created to please the artist's record buyers.

It's terribly hard to define a country record, other than saying, I know one when I hear one. I've given up trying since George Strait came out with "Marina Del Rey" more than a decade ago. But if you listen to Patty's "Only What I Feel," I think you'll find that every cut on that album, including "Blame It on Your Heart," is a country cut.

Among most of the female hit acts, a great song is a temptation they can't resist, no matter how it conflicts with the image they or their label are attempting to project. And one reason they can't resist is that most of them are such terrific singers that within reason they can sing almost anything. But of all of them, I think Patty stays consistently closer to traditional country. She does it with her voice and her choice of songs.

Roy Wunsch was right about Patty, and Patty was right about Patty. Her music is embedded in country tradition. That image comes honestly, both from her upbringing and from her early experiences so long ago on Music Row.

A number of years back, she recorded a great country classic called "If My Heart Had Windows." Later she told Vernell Hackett how she came to record the song. "At the time I was writing with Acuff-Rose, probably one of the first publishing companies in Nashville," she says. Acuff-Rose was not only one of the first, but also one of the best, founded by Hank Williams's mentor, Fred Rose, along with Grand Ole Opry great, Roy Acuff.

"They had this song and Ronnie Gant called me into his office and played it for me . . . It was a female version, a

Surrounded by fans.

girl had sung a demo of it, and I said, 'This is the old George Jones song!'

"He says, 'Yeah, it's been twenty years ago since he cut it.' And so I just took it home and sat around with it, started playin' it, and listened to George's version of it, and thought, hey, this is the kind of song I wanna do."

Ed Morris mentioned that Patty does not record her own songs, although she was signed as a songwriter long before she was ever signed as an artist. When an artist does not record her own songs it means one of two things: either she is not writing songs or the songs she is writing do not in her mind measure up to the songs coming in from the outside.

Back in the sixties, an era that spawned a lot of goofy ideas, it became an article of faith among pop fans that real artists, like Bob Dylan, the Rolling Stones, and the Beatles, write the songs they record. Supposedly that's an indication that they are baring their artistic souls to the rest of us. In the eighties that idea finally caught on in country music.

It's a ridiculous idea. Enrico Caruso did not sing his own songs. Frank Sinatra did not sing his own songs, and Elvis Presley did not sing his own songs, though his name turned up on some of them. And almost never does George Jones sing his own songs. It's a good thing, not a bad thing, that an artist of Patty's stature continues to take the objective approach to recording the songs that she and her husband-producer, Emory Gordy, feel are the best available. As this is being written, Patty has another top ten single with ''You Will,'' and she didn't write that one either. Her ''Only What I Feel'' album is well past gold. It looks like she's weathered the changes well.

11

Up and Coming

A NUMBER OF TALENTED WOMEN ARE POISED TO BREAK through into the top ranks of country singers. In fact, during the six or seven months between the book's completion and its publication, one or two or more may have done so. It is a measure of how far women have come in country that nearly all the major labels in Nashville have at least one female act they tout as the next Reba or Dolly. What follows is not meant to be a complete description of all the women with label deals who have a legitimate shot at country stardom, but is a sampling of the varied styles and personalities that will be changing the face of female country music in the months to come.

Keep in mind Pat Rolfe's observation that as this is being written, not a single female act has broken into the ranks of the big sellers since Trisha Yearwood back in 1991. It is entirely possible that women will gain a fairer share of executive positions in the Nashville music industry long before they see parity on the country charts.

There are more than a dozen record labels that are rated major competitors on the country scene. Only a few years ago, Warner Brothers was so far in front of the rest that they were like the old New York Yankees—strong, confident, and maybe even a little arrogant to some of the other labels that were seeing leaner times.

It's not that Warner Brothers has stumbled. Dwight Yoakam is hot. Travis Tritt is still hot. Randy Travis continues to sell a lot of records. But labels like MCA, Liberty, and Arista have racked up some mighty sales figures, and even Mercury, which was once considered Nashville's stepchild, among major labels, has made huge strides over the past two years.

In particular, while many other labels have developed major-selling women in recent years, Warner Brothers has not found a girl to take up where Emmylou Harris left off.

But that may be changing. As this book is being written, A & R Senior Vice President Martha Sharp is walking around with a gleam in her eye and a new quickness in her step. If you ask her why she is smiling, she will whisper two syllables: Faith Hill.

I asked her why Faith Hill has lowered her blood pressure and she sent me a note that included the following:

"Faith is my idea of the perfect artist. She's beautiful, talented, charismatic, and unbelievably self-directed. She lights up a room, a stage, or a video set. She learned a whole lot while working for Reba about taking charge of one's own career, and she's done that. We think she's a star."

Here's another woman taking charge of her career. It comes up again and again, and almost all the female stars either are already doing it or are on the road to doing it.

Faith Hill had it right from the beginning. Back in the late eighties she moved to Nashville after graduating from high school in Star, Mississippi, and went to work as a receptionist in the office of country star Gary Morris. According to a 1993 article in the Jackson (Mississippi) *Clarion-Ledger* by Leslie R. Myers, Morris heard her in the office singing along with the radio and asked her to sing on a demo for him.

"In Morris's office," said the article, "She met her men-

Faith Hill and songwriter Gary Burr.

tor, Gary Burr. Burr had Hill sing with him at Nashville's Bluebird club—where she was 'discovered' by a Warner Brothers vice president.''

Now, that story sounds like pure chance, the kind of luck that always happens to the other guy but not you. Pure chance it was not. It was savvy and instinct on the part of the young woman from Star, Mississippi.

In Nashville all kinds of good things happen to women who get jobs as secretaries and receptionists on Music Row, if only they can come across well to other people. They become publicists, A & R people, promotion people, and sometimes stars. Yes, it helps to be attractive.

What Faith Hill did right was go to where the music is (Nashville), get a job where the music is (a music company), and perform at one of Nashville's premier listening rooms. If you do that enough, sooner or later someone who matters in the music business is going to hear you. Then if you're really good, and that someone is in a receptive mood that night, then something good might happen.

By doing all those things, Faith Hill lessened the odds against her. The odds still weren't all that good that a record deal would come out of her efforts, just better than the odds against most folks out there struggling for a place on some label's roster. When I started writing this book, the odds still weren't all that good that stardom awaited her. As I looked at the Billboard country album charts, only four of the top twenty artists were females.

But Martha Sharp saw stardom in the future of Faith Hill. Martha had been right before, and she was right again. Faith's first single, "Wild One," was a number one country hit and as this is being written, her followup, "Piece Of My Heart," is country's hottest new single. It's just possible that Faith might be that brand new female star the industry has been waiting for.

Faith Hill was born Faith Perry in Jackson, Mississippi, which, in spite of the old song, is a pretty big town. She lived in a number of Mississippi towns before her parents settled in Star, which is a very small town. She started singing at the age of five "in churches, fairs, community centers, and rodeos across Mississippi," according to the *Clarion-Ledger* article. In short, singing was obviously what she has always wanted to do.

What a splendid opportunity she has to make it all happen.

Another artist who has lived music since her early childhood is Columbia's Joy White. Her album "Between Midnight and Hindsight" is a treat. Producers Blake Chancey and Paul Worley cut her as that rarest of country birds, the female singer of hard country music.

I have mentioned several times how female country stars seem to want to resist that classification. So we have yet to test what would happen if a female Randy Travis should come along. Joy White could be it if she wants to be and if Columbia stays with her. Her recordings are full of personality and country heart and soul.

She was born in Turrell, Arkansas, but was raised in Mishawaka, Indiana. Like Faith Hill, Joy White sang in churches as a child and sang at the family guitar pulls. In her label bio, she presents an interesting perspective concerning the music she heard on the radio as a child. "Country radio was playing in our house all the time but I didn't really like it much back then," she admits. "A lot of country in the '70s was very watered down, and they were slammin' out two albums a year! It's just not like that now."

Imagine a singer saying that she didn't like the country music she heard on the radio when she was a kid because it wasn't country enough! And she was right about where country was throughout much of the seventies. The seventies, especially the latter part of them, were a time when the music business was trying to make country music a surrogate for the discredited middle-of-the-road radio format that was supposed to attract all those high-spending middle-aged listeners.

In her teenage years Joy was a professional, singing with bands and doing jingles for local commercials. She was committed to what she was doing. School was an encumbrance, so she graduated from high school half a year before her class. Meanwhile, she had gone to school on the records of Linda Ronstadt, who she credits with being her primary influence. Fortunately, her style is too far from Linda's for anybody to recognize any cloning process.

She told Clark Parsons of the *Nashville Scene* about her early career in Nashville after she moved there in the early eighties.

"I was very young. I did things always backwards. I learned through making mistakes, putting my foot in my mouth, partying too much."

If you take a look at the cover of her "Between Midnight and Hindsight" CD you might get a feel for what she's talking about. She looks like someone who is used to saying whatever comes into her mind. Her day gigs never seemed

Joy White

to last too long either because, as she told Parsons, "I never liked having a boss tell me what to do."

But before long people were paying her to do demos. Demo singing is a strange world to be in. On one hand, people are paying you to "sell" the song you're singing to whomever the demos are being pitched. The star of the demo is supposed to be the song, not the singer, so the singer should not sound so distinctive that the producer, A & R person, etc., cannot imagine his or her artist singing the song. On the other hand, if the demo singer sounds really impressive, somebody who counts is bound to ask, "Who is that singer anyway?" And that's how unknowns sometimes get their first record deal.

Before long Joy was in such demand that she was singing on about ten demos a week. That's a lot for any demo singer, but especially for a female singer because, as you've already seen, there are a lot more male singers, and therefore a lot more songs being written for and pitched to male singers, and generally you don't hire a female singer to sing a song you intend to pitch to male singers.

So she was a hot item, and it was just a matter of time until somebody with a record label discovered her.

Back around 1989 she almost got her first record deal, with Capitol, which is now Liberty Records. But just when it looked right, some important new executives came into the company and others went. That is par for the course. Most artists experience a bunch of "almosts" before anything really good happens.

Enter Paul Worley, a still-young veteran producer who, at the time, was a publishing executive for Sony/Tree. Paul was producing hit records on Highway 101 and several people who were pitching him songs for the group were using Joy to demo them. Paul began to get interested in the Arkansas girl from Indiana.

The result of this frequent exposure was a record deal with Columbia, which is a member of the Sony Music family. Her first album is a very respectable effort, and although it has not taken the industry by storm, Sony will surely persevere with her, because on top of the raw talent, her delivery carries an urgent enthusiasm you don't hear all that often in country. Besides, she can sing very country when she chooses, and we need another woman who sings true country.

You will remember that Dolly Parton pointed her music in a pop direction at one point in her career, and Reba McEntire expanded her music far beyond the rodeo girl image early on. This next artist is a great singer who can do whatever material she chooses and do it well. But she chose to try pop for many years, and it cost her dearly.

Her name is Deborah Allen. Born in Memphis, she has been a fixture in Nashville since the seventies. Over the past two decades she and her husband, Rafe VanHoy, have created some of the finest music to come out of Nashville.

As songwriters, they have each had tremendous success, Rafe with great cowritten country hits like "Golden Rings," and "All My Old Flames Have New Names," while Deborah's songs have been recorded by Sheena Easton, Diana Ross, Conway Twitty, and Brenda Lee, to name but a few. In 1979 Deborah made a splash in a fairly bizarre way, by singing duets with the long-deceased Jim Reeves, or at least the recorded voice of the long-deceased Jim Reeves. In 1984 she struck gold as a solo artist with "Baby I Lied," which was top five on both the country and adult/contemporary charts and earned her two Grammy nominations and a nomination for the Horizon Award by the Country Music Association.

She had other chart successes too, but still, their target was the pop charts, and, for those who don't know, the pop industry is controlled by forces outside of Nashville and it is very hard to convince any L. A. executive that anybody in Nashville knows anything about pop music.

Well, it doesn't matter anymore. Much of what happens in pop music today is more of an event than it is music,

Deborah Allen at the Radio Seminar in 1993.

many musical people have fled L. A. for the Cumberland Basin in Middle Tennessee, and a lot of the music Deborah and Rafe made that would have been called pop years ago now falls comfortably within the realm of country music.

How, you may well ask, can country be absorbing old pop music if it is still riding a wave of traditionalism? The answer is that ever since country music became a commercial force it has traveled in several directions at one time. So it is not surprising that George Strait and Alan Jackson can coexist alongside Billy Ray Cyrus. Anyway, after her success in the eighties, which seemed to be taking Deborah in the right direction, she had considerable problems with her label, which was going through ''traumatic executive changes.''

But Rafe and Deborah never gave up. They pursued a number of projects and finally landed a deal with Giant Records, a new label associated with the Warner Brothers empire. Having always had one foot in country music, and feeling that country's boundaries have moved enough to take in her other foot, Deborah feels very comfortable with her new label.

Her first album on the label, ''Delta Dreamland,'' is loaded with strong songs, all cowritten by Deborah along with Rafe, her buddies Billy Burnette and Mark Collie, and long-time friend Bobby Braddock, one of the greatest songwriters ever to set foot on Music Row.

Rafe and Deborah decided to go out with their own sixteen-millimeter movie camera and shoot their own videos. The results, particularly on the first single, ''Rock Me,'' were stunning. While the singles off the album so far have garnered considerable airplay, we still await the breakthrough record.

By most measures Deborah Allen has had huge success in the music business. And yet her goal has always been to be a major recording star. She is one of those people with a talent so rich and a personality so filled with the joy of life that stardom seems inevitable.

But stardom is never inevitable. Stardom is one of the great mysteries of our society. It is only after it happens that the pundits always knew it would.

How about Carlene Carter? Is she a star, or isn't she? Just a couple of years back she had a major hit country single called ''I Fell in Love,'' and a few more sizable chart records, then nothing. She needed a new album; instead she became a cable video show host. Meanwhile three years elapsed between album releases.

But the wait is over. In the latter half of 1993 her new label, Giant, released her new album, ''Little Love Letters,'' sparking immediate action on the country scene. By late August her single, ''Every Little Thing,'' was number three on the Billboard hot country singles charts, and the album was taking giant steps up the album charts. You begin to get this feeling that somehow Carlene Carter is destined to be a big country star if she just keeps her foot on the accelerator and forgets that she ever wanted to be a rock and roll idol.

''Most of my stuff is really tongue-in-cheek and fun,''

Deborah Allen with Tanya Tucker.

Carleen Carter

she told journalist Robert Oermann in an article written for the *Tennessean* in August of '93. "I want to be healthy and happy. . . . I want to make people happy. I want people to hear me do my thing and smile. But there is a seriousness about me in that I want it all to sound good."

There was a time she didn't fit in at all. Like Deborah Allen, for a long time Carlene had her dreams fixed on the pop music world. Carlene was a rocker, and apparently there were record professionals in the pop world who were irresistibly drawn to the idea that the daughter of June Carter and country legend Carl Smith would turn out to be a rocker.

In the late seventies and early eighties she recorded five albums that excited the critics but left radio, and therefore the public, cold. She was still very young then, and maybe kind of out of control. She went through three marriages and fought drug problems for a time.

She's not so young anymore, closer to forty than to thirty, and the funny part about that is that among today's country women, that's a pretty good age to be.

Does Carlene really fit into country now?

"If anything, I'm kicking butt even harder than I was on some of the early albums. Fortunately it fits in now," she told Oermann. Which brings us back to that country music mystery we discussed before: how much is country music stretching out today to take in all those subgenres that have been cast out by the pop world? And how much of that crypto-pop can be incorporated into country music radio before country loses the identity that first started bringing fans back into the record stores?

That's not to say that Carlene does or does not belong in country. Only the country fans will decide that. Make no mistake about it, over the next ten years country music will change. It always does. Carlene's music is definitely one of the directions country may go. And if it does, she will be a major country act.

Sometimes a recording artist will get to a point where her career is hanging precisely in balance between stardom and close-but-keep-pluggin'. I believe that at the moment these words are being written, that's exactly where Shania Twain is.

First, who is Shania Twain? You pronounce the name "Shuh-NYE-uh," which is an Ojibway name. She is part Ojibway, through her father, and all Canadian. Mercury Records is very high on Shania, and they ought to be.

She was reared in Timmins, Ontario, and showed enough talent early on that at the age of three her mother would sit her up on restaurant counters to sing along with the jukebox for customers. Her family was poor, but when they had the money her mother would journey with her nine hours to Toronto for music lessons. By high school she was working steadily with local bands.

But she kept her singing career to herself, and she still doesn't like to run around advertising it. Maybe it's because it doesn't seem like real work compared to her former summer gig.

"From spring through fall I'd work with my father in the bush," she said. "I was foreman with a thirteen-man crew, many of whom were Indians. I'd run the crew, and we'd plant millions of trees through the summer. We'd get up between four and six in the morning, live on beans, bread and tea, walk up to an hour to the site, and work all day in rain, snow, or sunshine, in the middle of the bush, hours from civilization. I did that for five years. It was very hard work."

At the end of the summer she'd head for Toronto, toss her flannels and denims in the hamper, clean up, and slip into sequins to entertain the people.

When she was twenty-one, both her parents were killed in an automobile accident, and suddenly her entertainment career took on new meaning, because now she was responsible for her younger siblings.

Shania Twain

She spent years making a living as a performer in Canada before she decided to grab the country music brass ring in Nashville. Her friend and manager, Mary Bailey, got her together with Nashville attorney Dick Frank, who got her in touch with songwriter-producer Norro Wilson and Mercury associate Buddy Cannon. They cut a demo on her and played it for Harold Shedd, a Mercury senior vice president who has been vital in the making of Alabama, K. T. Oslin, and numerous other star country acts.

Shortly thereafter, Mercury signed Shania, and as record careers go that's pretty much of a no muss, no fuss, no bother entry into the world of country recording. But as hard as it is to get a record deal these days, that's the easy part compared to making the deal work. At this point in her career, a lot of folks have heard her on the radio, and she has sold a few albums.

Now comes the scary part. The dream always says, If only I can get a deal with a major record label, when the people hear me I'll be a star. But when you've come as far as Shania has come, you face a new set of realities. Do I really have a voice that sets me apart? Have I recorded a song that's so powerful that it can launch a career? When you start out you can only go forward. When you've made it onto the playlists of hundreds of key stations, then you can go forward or backward.

As this is written her album has just arrived on *Billboard's* country album charts. Now comes the first moment of truth. Will the people buy the CD's and cassettes in the record stores and off the K-Mart racks? If they do, her career is off to a flying start. If they don't, it's back to the long, laborious, sometimes frightening job of finding, or writing, the magic song or songs that will make the difference.

She does have the voice, she's got the look, she certainly has the guts to be a star. But the proof, as they used to say in the days of twelve-inch vinyl, is in the grooves.

As you can see by the pictures, most of the women on the major labels contending for country stardom meet our society's standards for being called "beautiful," which is perhaps too bad because it plays into this horrible rut we've gotten into concerning what women are supposed to look like.

Ronna Reeves

But for the time being we're stuck with our stereotypes and the effects they have on both men and women, and the next one in this chapter certainly looks beautiful. Fortunately she has the rest of what it takes to be a major country artist.

Her name is Ronna Reeves. Like Shania Twain she had a single that every country fan heard on the radio and put her *this* close to breaking out of the pack.

This young Texan started out by singing along with the radio just like the rest of us. From then on she went her own way. When she was eight years old she was Little Miss Big Spring. At the age of eleven she had her own group and soon she was playing venues like the Brand New Opry in Odessa, the Grapevine Opry, and Billy Bob's.

In country music, Texas is its own country. Besides furnishing Nashville with many of country's greatest stars, Texas has its own ideas about who America's greatest singers are. Throughout the rest of America George Strait is a

Ronna Reeves and Sammy Kershaw at FanFair in 1992.

big Star. In Texas George Strait is a god.

So when promoters Ron and Joy Cotton called to ask her to open for Strait, she must have thought she'd been called to heaven. Instead, she opened for George for a year and a half and then began working shows with artists like Garth Brooks, Randy Travis, and Reba McEntire.

Soon she was making trips to Nashville, and eventually she found her way over the walls, under the fences, and onto the Mercury roster. Her first album was ''The More I Learn,'' and the title cut did so well on the radio and the charts that Ronna and Mercury must have felt that major success was but a moment away.

Like most of the other artists in this chapter, however, she is still looking for a single so powerful that it will jerk country fans to their feet and drag them into the stores by the hundreds of thousands.

Ask any country artist about the record business these days and he or she is certain to say, "It's a jungle out there," or, "It's a mean cruel world," or, "Every day's another fight for life"—you get the picture. The competition is fierce. There's no easy road to a hit and no easy road once you've got a hit.

Mercury has another young female artist they're trying to steer through the jungle. Her name is Shelby Lynne, and she records for their Morgan Creek affiliate. As this is being written *Billboard* is sending mixed signals about Shelby's near future. The album, titled "Temptation," is highlighted as the "Pacesetter" album with a fifteen-place leap on the country album charts. Her single, "Feelin' Kind of Lonely Tonight," is going nowhere, however. Try to figure it all out. I can't.

Shelby Lynne has already earned considerable accolades. In 1991, the Academy of Country Music selected her as country music's Best New Female Artist. Meanwhile, the critics were competing for extravagant phrases of praise.

"This girl can sing the chrome off a trailer hitch," *USA Today*'s fine music writer, David Zimmerman, wrote. And the ubiquitous Robert Oermann wrote in the *Tennessean*, "Voices like this come along once in a generation. . . . With her flame-thrower delivery, you know you're listening to someone special." And according to her label bio, Tammy Wynette called her "the best voice in country music."

Is this hype, or is she really that good?

She's very good. Her voice has range, dynamics, personality, and style. She's powerful. She's passionate. She's accurate. She's terrific. And she's already had three albums that have drawn a lot of critical acclaim without breaking her out of the pack.

And now comes "Temptation," produced by Brent Maher, who has a track record for writing great songs and producing great recordings.

They've come up with something special, whether the album continues to zoom up the charts or drops like a brick next week.

"We went for more of an Irving Berlin lyric with a Bob Wills beat," she says. "And you know what Bob Wills said—'It ain't music if you can't dance to it.' "

So they sat down with Jamie O'Hara, known best by the public as half of the O'Kanes but known on music row as a great songwriting stylist. Maher and O'Hara came up with some distinctive material. They added a handful of songs from other sources that fulfilled their concept, and they went into the studio with an eighteen-piece band, including nine horns. The result is a fabulous album, a calculated gamble by a terrific talent.

Why a gamble? There's a lot of western swing on this album, and in spite of occasional hits over the years, neither radio nor the folks have been all that friendly to western swing since the big band sound faded out in the late forties. Back in the mid-seventies at Tree Publishing Company there was a producer named Tommy Allsup who believed that western swing was ready for a comeback. He went into the studio and produced a lot of it. And most of it was very good. Both he and Tree had power in the music business but there was no swing revival in the offing.

Not then, so why now?

Because country fans are supposed to be into dance music, and swing music above all is dance music.

There's another dimension to this album. There's more than swing here. It has a lot of romance and its songs echo the quality of Tin Pan Alley classics, much of which was lost when rock and roll took over pop music. For years pop music has begged for a return to the kinds of melodies and lyrics that tugged at the heartstrings of our parents and grandparents, catchy phrases they sang to themselves as they walked down the street (back in the days when people still walked down the street). It wouldn't be at all surprising if the mass revival of the traditional pop song came out of Nashville. After all, Nashville is the only music center left in the country where the song is still more important than the production.

Music Row is not paradise on earth. But some of what the entertainment media says about Nashville's narrow music focus should be taken with a grain of salt—or a pound of it.

And now, Martina McBride. Back in 1991 she was selling T-shirts at Garth Brooks concerts. A year later she was the opening act on Garth's shows. That's the way it goes in the music business. Rarely.

She started out making music professionally at an early age with her father's family band, the Schiffters. She sang and played keyboard with them as they worked their weekend gigs in the neighborhood of their home town, Sharon, Kansas. They were a popular band in their part of Kansas, and neighbors looked forward to seeing them as they worked their way around.

Her dad had a strong traditional country background, so she was conditioned early by her father's favorites, the Hanks: Hank Snow, Hank Thompson, and Waylon (''Are You Sure Hank Done It This Way'') Jennings.

After she graduated from high school she toured with a number of bands, then moved to Wichita, where she met her future husband, John McBride, who owned a sound company.

In a *Tune-In* article written by Carl Bradley back in 1992 she said something that gives the reader a fine insight on the attitude that some artists bring to the business. ''I'm an optimist, and I didn't really sit and go, 'Wow, this is a hard row to follow,' . . . I never let myself consider that it couldn't happen. I just thought, 'Okay, I'm going to go for it, and I'll give it as long as it takes.' And I never even considered doing anything else. I'm thankful that this worked out, because I don't know what I would have been doing in five to ten years. I didn't prepare myself for anything else. I just single-mindedly focused on pursuing a career as a performer.''

Martina McBride at her FanFair debut.

After she and John were married they spent a lot of time plotting their future course in the music business. "After awhile, we decided to really get focused and go after a record deal," she told Bradley. "The first thing that we needed to do was make a good demo tape and pitch it to the record companies. I needed good material to sing, and it's really hard to get good material over the phone when you're calling from Kansas. We took a trip to Nashville in August of '89 to find material. We realized that if we wanted to be serious about country music this [Nashville] is the place you have to live. So we moved."

Music trade magazine *Radio & Records* described how she got her RCA deal in their May 8, 1990, issue. "After moving to Nashville in 1990, McBride immediately recorded a five-song demo and began shopping it around. She received some initial interest, but nothing happened. Meanwhile, John took a job as Garth Brooks's sound man. To be near her husband, McBride took a job selling Brooks T-shirts.

"She began doing demo work after friend/session player Mike Chapman introduced her at publishing companies around town. Relentless in shopping her own demo, McBride found out RCA wouldn't take unsolicited material. So she wrote 'requested material' on an envelope containing her tape. When the label's Randy Talmadge and Josh Leo heard it, she won a record deal."

Before you artist hopefuls start mailing in demo tapes with "requested material" on it, let it be known that most A & R people are wise to that dodge. Also, before you consider that it's a great idea to pursue stardom without ever wondering what you might do if you fail, consider that Martina hasn't made it big yet.

But she might. Her current album, "The Way That I Am," is a very stylish platform for her powerful, expressive vocals. A single off that album, "My Baby Loves Me," was a big airplay hit and her followup, "Life #9," appears to be duplicating that success.

Martina McBride on tour with Garth Brooks.

Another thing she has going for her: young as she is, Martina is coproducer on "The Way That I Am."

"I had a lot of input on what musically it was going to sound like," she told her label biographer, "not only the vocal tone but the instrumentation, arrangements, just different ideas here and there. That's the only way I can work. It's hard for me to understand just coming in and singing the songs, letting somebody else do all the overdubs and not having an input into the end product. I need to have a lot of input so an album will reflect me as an artist. Since I don't write [songs] that's where my creative outlet is." What we see here is an artist who is attempting to assert some control over her music early in her career.

She has attracted a lot of attention in the music business

with her first two albums, and quite a few music folks expect her to be a big act.

RCA is working hard at breaking another talented female artist, Lari White. A native of Dunedin, Florida, she caught a strong gust of gospel music through her grandfather, who was a Primitive Baptist preacher. Soon she was performing at churches and festivals as part of the White Family Singers. Like a number of other women in this chapter, Lari knew at an early age that music would be her career.

At the University of Miami she majored in music engineering and moonlighted in music. "At night I'd sing in Top 40 bands, jazz bands, and big bands," she told her label biographer, "and days I'd be in the studio doing background vocals and jingles. . . . I even sang salsa commercials and did a Toyota Corolla commercial in Spanish."

Her last six months in college she began writing songs. Then, after graduation, she visited the music scenes of Los Angeles, Chicago, and New York. In the spring of 1988, Lari came to Nashville to audition for TNN's "You Can Be a Star." Not only did she pass her audition, she won the talent contest, and the money that went with it helped to finance her first year in Nashville.

"I spent my first year in Nashville just writing and taking my demo tapes around," she said, but she loved Nashville, even when the weather turned cold and she found herself facing the first real winter of her life. Along came a record deal from Capitol, which is what every artist dreams of, but like many first record deals, it was short-lived and unfruitful.

Then for a year and a half she performed in various Nashville theater venues, but music was her real home. One night in 1991 she did an ASCAP showcase. Rodney Crowell was at the show, was impressed, and happened to need a backup singer for his summer tour. While they were working together he suggested that they produce some sides on her together, and they did. The result was her present RCA deal and Lari's first album, "Lead Me Not."

There are some lessons to be gleaned from this story, which is not yet a success story but which may well prove to be. If you're trying to make it in a music town, get on the stage as much as you can. The experience will make you a better singer and you never can tell who might be in the audience. Also, these days, as you have seen, some producers try to get artists involved in the entire process, from picking songs and writing them, to coproducing them. Lari White was ready for all of these because she had done so much before she even arrived in Nashville.

The title song of her album hung around the *Billboard* country singles chart for many weeks, but the album itself has not taken off. The songs on the album, many of them written or cowritten by Lari, represent a versatile mix of material. Whether that makes for a very interesting variety or an album that points out no direction for the artist depends on the listener. There is no doubt about her talent. But the competition is sturdy, so I guess we'll have to wait to see what'll happen that will catapult Lari White or one of her competitors into the top rank of female country singers.

There are a number of other new female country acts battling for a place on the crowded playlists of radio and the limited shelves of store racks. I have provided a sampling to give you an idea of who to look out for in the near future.

It's a frustrating time to be an emerging female artist. Although there are a record number of women drawing gold and platinum sales, it seems hard for the new ones to break through. Men still overwhelmingly dominate the singles charts. In fact, as this is being written, the only females with a top twenty single on the *Billboard* country chart are Patty Loveless, Suzy Bogguss, and Mary Chapin Carpenter.

Why? Is radio resisting female artists? If their records

are so good, why don't they get played? The answers to those questions are, I don't know and I don't know. Radio gets accused of a lot of things and sometimes they get a bum rap. Is the music these women are making all that good? I think so, but maybe the fans don't. Maybe the female fans don't.

12

Lorrie Morgan

OF THE HOT FEMALE COUNTRY ACTS TODAY, TWO ARE the daughters of country stars. They are, of course, Pam Tillis and Lorrie Morgan.

You may assume that being the son or the daughter of a star can make it easier for an artist to become a star, but such an assumption is not necessarily correct. That's because being the progeny of a star or former star might help get you through the door, but no matter what you may have heard, getting through the door is the easy part.

Getting through the door means getting a label executive to sit still long enough to hear a tape. That's generally easy for the child of a star because of his/her parents' connections. The child herself may well have connections because she will have rubbed shoulders with record executives in the course of her parent's recording career. But *that* only gets her through the door.

There was a time years ago when record executives would sign an artist to do a friend a favor. That hardly ever happens anymore. The stakes are too high. The money's too big. Today when an act gets signed it means that somebody really believes in it. So it doesn't matter who your daddy is; if you're gonna get a record deal you're gonna have to earn it.

And getting the record deal isn't the hard part either. The

really hard part is pleasing the public. The public does not care who is the artist's daddy. The public cares what the artist sounds like on the radio, on the cassette, or on the CD. Every year record labels sign dozens of artists. They all make their deals with high hopes, but very few of them make it.

Both Pam and Lorrie had record deals that failed. Both of them kept on plugging, and both have since become major stars.

Lorrie is the daughter of golden-throated George Morgan. Although George sang beautifully, he was not a superstar. Back in 1949, which is a lifetime ago, he had a million-selling hit called "Candy Kisses," and he never came close to duplicating that success. He was a member of the Grand Ole Opry for many years, but Opry membership does not translate into success in the record business. No doubt it did help her get her first appearance on the Opry when she was a teenager.

"My thirteen-year-old knees were absolutely knocking," Lorrie says, "but I saw Dad standing there just bawling, and those people gave me a standing ovation. I thought, 'This is what I'm doing the rest of my life.' I thought it was going to be that easy. Little did I know."

The average country fan reading that statement might be a little skeptical. To him or her an appearance on the Opry at thirteen seems a lot like having it made. But people in the music industry are aware that the Opry has little bearing on a recording career and the big venue personal appearances that come *after* the first big hit records.

Many years ago the premier publishing company was Acuff-Rose. Like every single major publishing company born in Nashville, Acuff-Rose has been sold to an out-of-town company, in this case Gaylord, the entertainment company that also owns the Opry, Opryland, the Opryland Hotel, WSM radio, and The Nashville Network.

"I started writing and got on as a writer at Acuff-Rose," Lorrie says "and from there I went on to be their receptionist. I did a lot of demo sessions during my lunch hour

Lorrie Morgan

and after work. Any time they asked me to do a demo, I would do it.''

Acuff-Rose had a record label called Hickory, which at one time had actually had hit records in both the country and pop fields. Lorrie got signed to Hickory, but by that time the label's best days were behind it, and her chances of striking big with them were just about nil.

She found herself, year after year, doing the things artists do who are hanging in there, hoping somehow that something good might happen. She toured with her father until he died, in 1975, and as a solo act, traveling with her mom and one other musician, playing with house bands, which is a very hard way to go. She toured with George Jones and performed at Opryland. She appeared on the Opry and The Nashville Network whenever she could, and continued writing songs and doing demos—anything to stay in the ballgame while she pursued the elusive record deal.

Lorrie with Barry Beckett, the producer of many of her RCA hits.

And then came RCA Records. When they signed her, they teamed her up with veteran producer Barry Beckett. As a team they clicked almost immediately.

"He's very calming," she told Vernell Hackett. "He doesn't get overexcited and he's very understanding in the studio. He listens a lot to my opinions and that helps a lot, you know, you're not just a dumb blonde singer, you've got some knowledge . . . Barry has really taught me a lot in the studio too because I was always real hyper in the studio . . .''

But, professionally speaking, it was not love at first sight. ''As a matter of fact, when I first met Barry it was very bad vibes. RCA had a couple of producers in mind and Barry was one of the first ones that I had a meeting with. We played him some songs from a session that I had done previously for RCA, just a spec session that got me the deal.''

Spec is short for speculation or speculative. In studios and among musicians there are basically two fee schedules, master session pay and demo session pay. When an artist is looking for a label deal, she goes out and finds or writes the best songs she can; then she or her producer or backer or whatever book the studio, the engineer and the musicians.

The artist or whoever is backing her is spending a lot of money hoping against odds that some record company will like the session and sign her. In order to cut down on the money being gambled, whoever is paying for the session books the musicians, studio, and engineer at spec rates, which are generally demo rates with the promise that if the artist gets a record deal and the session is used by the label, then everybody involved will get master session rates.

Anyway, Lorrie was playing the cuts on her spec session for producer Barry Beckett.

''And Barry listened to them and he said, 'You know, I don't believe a word of it.' It made me mad, although it was true, 'cause the songs that were recorded were not me at all. And he knew that [but] I was just very upset, and I thought, well how dare he come in and say something like that, even though it was true and I knew it was true.

''The next meeting we showed him videos, about forty-five minutes of tape, of live performances on the Opry and *Nashville Now*, and he watched the whole tape . . . Barry set here lookin' over his glasses at the TV and they turned it off and he sat here for a second and he said, 'Now, I'm convinced.' I think he figured out that part of the reason [he was convinced that she was a potential star] was I had full control of the songs that I did on those tapes, and it makes a difference when you're in there singin' something you wanna sing instead of something that someone's telling you to sing.

"From then on we got along great."

They turned out to be a great team, Lorrie and Barry Beckett. She got eight top ten singles out of her first two albums, "Leave the Light on," and "Something in Red." Both albums have sold so well that they quickly moved her into the top rank of female country stars.

Smack in the middle of this star-making process, or maybe it was more toward the beginning, Keith Whitley died.

Keith was something special. He was obviously one of those committed, hard country artists who was on his way to major stardom. In 1988 he had three number one singles. The next year he was dead of an alcohol overdose. Lorrie and Keith had been married close to three years at the time of his death, which left her with their son, and a daughter from a previous marriage.

"My whole world revolved around Keith and the kids," Lorrie told Neil Pond in a 1991 article for *Country America*. "All I could think of was, 'What a waste, what a waste.' . . . I really didn't know if I was going to survive, I really didn't."

At the time of Keith's death her career was looking promising but was by no means assured. She had to control her grief and shock and survivors' guilt, stay strong for the kids, and cope with the tremendous stresses involved with building a music career. She had been striving for a long time just to get this far, and she was enough of a veteran in the business to know that if this opportunity didn't work, the next one might be a long time coming.

"There were many days when I thought I was going to give up," she told Pond. "But with the two kids I couldn't

*Lorrie with her husband Keith and family at
Nashville Memorial Hospital.*

do that. They needed a mother. That kind of grounded me.
I did it for them. I had to pull myself up by my bootstraps
and tell myself 'You *will* go on. You *will* continue.' ''

After Keith's death, Lorrie's career really began to take
off. Besides her platinum sales and her numerous hit singles, Lorrie has been a force on the key country award
shows over the past few years. In 1990 she and Keith received a Country Music Association award for Vocal Event
of the Year. That year she was nominated for Female Vocalist of the Year and the Horizon Award by the Country
Music Association and Female Artist of the Year and Star
of Tomorrow by TNN-Music City News Awards.

In 1991 Lorrie was again nominated by the CMA for
Female Vocalist of the Year and with Keith won Video
Collaboration of the Year at the TNN-Music City News
Awards.

In 1992 the Academy of Country Music nominated her in the Top Female Vocalist category.

With all this activity there is no doubt that Lorrie has made it to the top echelon of female country singers.

But Lorrie Morgan left RCA for BNA. She also switched producers and management. From the outside it appears that Lorrie, like Reba and Dolly, is very much in charge of her own career.

And her career is, first and foremost, singing songs. She told Vernell Hackett her approach to recording a song.

"I think the first thing you try and do is . . . make it your song. And that might not be exactly how it was arranged on the demo . . . I think you can turn a lot of songs around into your own . . . different arrangements, different tempos, the way you sing 'em kind of makes them your own song."

As you might guess from watching her on Country Music Television, the camera is her friend.

"I love doing videos," she told Vernell awhile back. "And the main reason I love doing them is because the director I had [on two of her videos], Steven Buck, was absolutely a joy to work with. When I first met Steven— of course they told me he was from L. A. and that scared me to death 'cause here's this guy who's worked around all these actors and actresses, and I've never done any actin' and I'm comin' in here, gonna be cold turkey, and he's gonna think I'm crazy.

"So when I first met him I said, 'Just wanna get one thing straight, right now, I'm a singer, not an actress. Don't yell at me, I'll get nervous. Be calm with me, be very understanding and we'll get along fine.' Boy was he great. . . .

"Sometimes these directors don't understand that you're a singer and not an actress and they bring 'em in here and they expect you to be Katherine Hepburn and people like that and that's not our deal, we're just tryin' to get our message across in video."

Her video experiences in front of the cameras must have given her a whole lot more confidence about the film me-

Lorrie at the Keith Whitley Memorial softball tournament.

dium, because last year she made it to the small screen in a made-for-TV movie, *Proudheart*.

The movie was produced by TNN—only its second attempt at filmmaking in its decade of existence. The script was selected especially for her. And she did a bang-up job in the role of a woman who returns to her hometown to bury the father she loved, mend fences with her nutty mother, and rehabilitate her father's garage business.

Just as fans misunderstand the lives of country music stars and their children, Lorrie grew up with misapprehensions about the lives of movie stars.

"When you're looking from the outside in," she told Sandy Smith of the *Tennessean*, "you perceive things a lot different than they really are. And growing up, I always thought the actresses and actors had these great lifestyles and were treated like kings and queens on the sets. I was in for a rude awakening."

Meanwhile, her recording career has continued to prosper. Her first album on BNA, "Watch Me," quickly went gold and since has gone platinum. Her new producer is Rich Landis, who has produced Juice Newton, the Oak Ridge Boys, Eddie Rabbitt, and Vince Gill, among others.

Lorrie Morgan has been through a lot, to say the least. She lost her father, and performing partner, during her adolescent years. She fought for years to get a major record deal. The record industry probably thought of her as an Opry brat and therefore did not take her seriously, so the road that eventually led her to RCA must have been a very rough one. Once she had her deal, but before she could establish a strong beachhead as an artist, her husband died under particularly harrowing circumstances.

She persevered, and succeeded.

Any female country artist has to be tough to make it to the top and stay there for any length of time. For Lorrie to have done what she has done, she must be one particularly tough cookie.

13

Tanya Tucker

WHAT A CAREER SHE HAS HAD! SHE'S BEEN A STAR for twenty-two years and she's still younger than most of her fellow platinum and gold women singers. Her story is the kind of longshot stuff that just doesn't happen to real people.

Imagine desert winds blowing dust around a house trailer in Utah. Inside a creaky air conditioner fails to cool the trailer. A girl is singing "Don't Come Home A-Drinkin'." Her face is that of a child but her voice is filled with knowledge.

An American automobile of considerable antiquity, perhaps an old Ford Galaxy, flies down the road in a swirl of gray dust and comes to a sliding halt by the trailer. Out jumps a man who races into the trailer and flourishes eleven hundred dollars that he has won at the Las Vegas gambling tables. "C'mon, girl!" he shouts, picking her up and whirling her around. "We're goin' to Vegas and get you a singing career!"

So off they go, rent a studio, and blow the money on producing a demo to send to Nashville. A few months later they are in Nashville, about to launch a legendary country recording career.

It probably didn't happen that way, but by Hollywood

Tanya Tucker performs at the age of 15.

standards, it might *sorta* happened that way. At least that's one story.

Another is that CBS Records' legendary producer Billy Sherrill was visiting Las Vegas when he ran into a hit song-writer named Dolores Fuller who wanted to talk to him about a thirteen-year-old girl named Tanya.

According to this version of the story, Fuller sent a tape to Sherrill in Nashville, and the next time Sherrill was in Las Vegas he told Tanya and her father Beau that if he ever found the right song for her he'd love to record her. Maybe he meant to do a kissoff, but Fuller was persistent.

"Dolores *just wouldn't leave me alone,*" he said. "She actually *drove me* into signing her."

And here's what happened once they did make it to Nashville. The company was CBS, and the producer was

Sherrill, the hottest music man in Nashville during the early seventies. He had launched the hit-making careers of Tammy Wynette, Barbara Mandrell, and Johnny Paycheck, and brought the careers of George Jones and Charlie Rich to new heights. He was going to work his recording magic on a thirteen-year-old girl.

As he often did, he contacted his favorite songwriters in town and let them know that he had this youngster he intended to make into a star. They scratched their heads and some of them probably thought he had lost his mind. What, Mandrell wasn't young enough? What were they supposed to do, try and write nursery rhymes for the kid?

Some of them did, or at least tried to come up with songs about first love and innocence, etc., and pitched them to Sherrill for Tanya, but her voice had about as much to do with innocence as Lauren Bacall's. The song that did it for Tanya, the very first release, was "Delta Dawn," a grim narrative about a broken woman. "Delta Dawn" was never pitched to him at all, Sherrill recalled. The night before he was scheduled to record her, goes this story, Sherrill was sitting at home watching the Johnny Carson Show and maybe wondering why he hadn't cancelled the session when he hadn't found any songs for her that absolutely killed him.

Bette Midler came out on Carson's stage and, as luck would have it, sang "Delta Dawn." Way back in 1972, country music was still a singles-oriented business, and Tanya's first single sold over three hundred thousand copies, which was very hot stuff then. She followed it up with hits like "Jamestown Ferry," "What's Your Mama's Name," and "Blood Red and Goin' Down," all story-type songs with a lot of emotion in them, and Tanya delivered every time.

In 1974 Tanya's contract with CBS was up and her father-manager Beau, not being the sentimental type, said goodbye to Billy Sherrill and took Tanya over to MCA Records, where the money was greener. There she continued to have hits.

Tanya with Roy Clark in 1975.

In 1978 MCA put out Tanya's "TNT" album, featuring a cover of her in a skintight thing holding a smoking fistful of dynamite behind her back. The message was clear. Tanya was no longer a precocious storyteller in song. She was now hot stuff.

Tanya was by that time making her own tastes known, and her tastes were a little more rockin' than her image. She hired some L. A. management, which is what upwardly mobile country acts tried to do in the late seventies, before sophisticated, street-smart management companies began to appear on Music Row. The "TNT" album was certified gold by the RIAA, a record industry organization that does such things, and Tanya climbed to a new plateau that lasted into the mid-eighties. Then for awhile she didn't have a label deal, but according to Paul Moore, who has been her booking agent at William Morris for over a decade, she worked steadily and successfully without a record deal.

In 1986 she signed with Capitol Records, which in Nashville is now called Liberty. Her producer was Jerry Crutchfield, who had produced many of her MCA records. Of her first twenty-one singles on Capitol/Liberty, all but two were top ten. Fifteen of them made it to top five. And she headed into the 1990s with her first platinum album, "What Do I Do With Me."

Then in 1991, almost twenty years after her first single hit the top of the charts, she was named the Country Music Association's Female Vocalist of the Year. The country music world gave a collective sigh and said, "It's about time now, isn't it?"

Tanya Tucker has actually had three separate recording careers representing three separate eras of country music. Her Billy Sherrill days date back to the Paleozoic era of country music when the giants that built Music Row still ran it and counted their successes a hundred thousand singles at a time.

Then she moved over to MCA and enjoyed some big album success when suburban fans discovered her during country music's outlaw-urban cowboy era. Her music changed from traditional, story-oriented country to a more rhythmic brand during that time.

That was the era when country music almost became middle America's music, but it took the new traditional explosion of the last five or six years to break down the final provincial barriers, and once again Tanya is a strong force in country music.

It is amazing for any female artist to stay at the top of the country charts as long as Tanya has, but when you consider that her personal life is most unconventional for a female country singer, then her success defies explanation.

Tanya has two children, a girl called Presley, named after you know who, and a boy called Beau, named after you know who if you've read this chapter. The father of her children is Ben Reed, an actor who has never been married

to her and whose career takes him to both coasts but seldom to Nashville. In *KNIX Country Spirit* magazine, back in 1992, Tanya talked about her relationship with the father of their children.

"The only way he could have it better," she told the interviewer, Sandy Lovejoy, "would be if he could see [the kids] a lot. They've got grandparents that love 'em; we're not divorced and fightin' over 'em. I told him that he should really be thankful for a lot of things."

According to the interview, Tanya would like to have another child, but under different circumstances. "I'm not gonna do anymore of this until I find the right man," she told Lovejoy.

What makes all this especially interesting is that in a business where artists and label heads still fear the effects of moral controversy on their record sales, Tanya's career has not appeared to have suffered. The day Beau was born was the day she was unavailable to pick up the CMA Female Vocalist of the Year Award that she had won. The award was very popular among many in the country music community. She had been nominated six times previously and many felt she was overdue for recognition.

Tanya seems to have something that might be called country common sense. Some time back Vernell Hackett did an interview with Tanya in which she explored her business relationship with her father, Beau, whose determination to make her a star was certainly a major factor in her early arrival on the country recording scene. At times he has acted as her manager, and at times she has hired outside management, but he always remains part of her business life.

"Sometimes we have a yell and a holler at each other but he's usually right if I've got everything together if I'm thinking straight and if I sit down and think about something for awhile he's usually right but there have been times it goes back and forth . . ." she told Vernell.

"But for most he's pretty right, he's pretty right. As far as knowing people and how to deal with 'em and some of

Tanya backstage with Clint Black.

the moves to make. But I disagree with him on a lot of angles. But I'd rather disagree with him than somebody else.''

Tanya also gave Vernell a glimpse of how she feels about herself as a singer. ''I don't and never have [considered myself a great singer]. I know people come to me and compliment me and say things I can't even say it embarrasses me and I'm thinking, well, I can't see it but I'm glad you can. You know it's not important that I see it, it's only important that I feel they're being honest with me . . . and I'm gonna keep on doing what I do and hope to God that I want everybody to love me that's my problem.

''It's like I understand I'm not a great singer and I don't understand why people think I am but [by] the same token I hate it when somebody says I ain't a good singer. I've never heard anybody say that or something detrimental about my singing. I've heard [someone] say that song was crappy but her voice is great. But I've never heard anybody call me a bad singer. But if they said anything I would probably be offended.''

Beneath her nearly impenetrable prose is an honesty so transparent you could weep. Being an entertainer means pleasing the people you entertain. You want them to think good things about you and you fear that they won't.

Recording artists have more than just the fans to worry about. At one point Tanya talked about what it feels like when you and your record label don't see eye to eye.

"I mean you could lay your guts out on vinyl . . . and it doesn't matter. And therefore you start feeling depressed like you're no good. I mean you get those feelings and pretty soon you're down, you're dancing as fast as you can. You're down on the bottom of the floor as far as your mental capacity and mental state and it's a shame that big business can do that to you. Yeah that's the down side and right now I'm on the up side and I hope to stay that way.''

Tanya's response had to do with a song she had cowritten that she had thought was very good, but which her record label would not release. She felt very close to the song and wanted her fans to get to hear it but her label would not cooperate and that hurt her.

Tanya is unlike many other female artists in that she spends a lot of time with the songwriters on Music Row, sometimes writes with them, and feels very much a part of their world.

"It's just *amazing* 'cause most of my friends are songwriters in the business. A few of 'em are entertainers but most of 'em are songwriters and that's who I hang out with. That's where I got my crazy reputation I guess—I don't know. These crazy songwriters . . . I get in a room with a bunch of writers and I just [get] the itch I just got to write something, you know. And I can be sitting in a room with them writing songs or playing songs that they've written and get three other ideas for another song. So that's what

I like about it 'cause I can really create.''

And how does Tanya Tucker relate to the public image of the wild and crazy Tanya Tucker?

''Well, it's very simple. I like to have a good time and enjoy being around my friends and when I do I get loud and crazy. And I love that and my mother always used to say don't laugh so loud and I'd say when I laugh with all the pain and sorrow in the world today when I laugh I want everybody to hear it.

''But there is a serious side to me and a very business side to me. I think [that] as you get a few years on you it's just natural.''

It's been a long haul for Tanya but it would seem that she has many miles to go. She had something of a childhood, but her career deprived her of an adolescence. Vernell asked her if she missed not having a normal teenager's life.

''No, I never felt like I missed anything. I felt like I gained a lot. I mean I wanted to get started when I was nine. I was upset I didn't get started then. Danny Davis will attest that he heard me when I was nine and that he wanted the record label to sign me . . . he said Chet Atkins wanted it but the [RCA] New York office wouldn't go for it at nine years old. . . . I'm sure I missed a few things but I don't think the things I've missed have been school or any of that stuff. It's always—I've missed a few things in the business. . . .

''I was unafraid when I was younger . . . one of the things I miss sometimes is that I get ready to go out in front of an audience, an award show, or something where all your peers are there and I'm going like, 'God I'm nervous' and I'm thinking I didn't use to be this way. . . . Youth is wonderful because you're unafraid, you just plow right in no matter if it's right or wrong or indifferent.''

It's interesting to note that someone like Trisha Yearwood could have been the girl next door to us with dreams of stardom, but not Tanya. Tanya was so young when she

Tanya and her children.

started chasing her future that she didn't really have a chance to dream it.

But there is at least one dream within the industry that she discussed with Hackett. And that is some day to work

Tanya at FanFair in 1992.

again with the man who produced her first hit records, Billy Sherrill.

As this book is written Tanya is riding another wave of success, this time care of a hit single with Delbert Mc-Clinton called ''Tell Me About It.'' In the meantime her onetime mentor Sherrill is not doing a lot. Reclusive, never one to run out and promote himself, Sherrill was at one time the king of record producers in Nashville. His greatest strength was knowing a hit song when he found it, which is a very rare talent. His low profile today is largely self-imposed. He is so talented he could produce hit records in any era. And Tanya has never forgotten the man who put together her first hit records. If you can follow the Tanya-ese, you'll see that there's a longing to go back to those early days in the studio with Billy when, unbelievably, a showbiz child became an overnight star.

"I know Billy and you know a man of his reputation and his talent and I mean I really was lucky to get him as a producer . . . not saying it would be lucky for anyone else because Billy's personality is not one that a lot of people think is copacetic. I mean you get along with him or you don't. And we had a rapport that was incredible. And you know I hear to this day he's still trying to find that and replace that and I have never tried to replace him. I've always wanted to have a great producer but I never could replace Billy Sherrill. But I hear that he's just been constantly searching for someone like me and I'd like to eventually maybe go back in and do another album with him. I'd love to."

There is not another one out there like Tanya Tucker. She means more to the country music world than most country fans suspect. She has been a talented survivor in the tough world of country hitmaking for more than two decades and she has learned so much about her business that if she can keep it all together she might make it through another two decades on the charts.

14

Suzy Bogguss

As I've mentioned earlier, it's interesting to note the different circumstances under which these women grew up. You could put them fairly easily into one of two categories, those who grew up like most of the rest of us and those who didn't.

On one hand we have Dolly, who grew up in humble Appalachia, Tanya, who went directly from house trailers to child star status, and Celinda Pink, who grew up in circumstances so disastrous it's a wonder she grew up at all. On the other side we have Trisha Yearwood, daughter of professionals, Mary Chapin Carpenter, Ivy Leaguer, and Suzy Bogguss.

Suzy grew up in Aledo, Illinois, the county seat of Mercy County, which is on the Mississippi River, just a little south of Rock Island, Illinois, and Davenport, Iowa.

Suzy must have gotten along well in her high school years. She was a cheerleader and homecoming queen and most women grow up knowing about the popularity contests those honors entail.

She attended Illinois State University and earned a bachelor's degree in metalsmithery, but music was what she wanted to do. She performed on the road for awhile and then in 1985 she arrived in Nashville. Two years later she was performing at Dollywood when she was found and signed to a record deal at Capitol Records.

The head of Capitol at the time was Jim Foglesong, who we met earlier in this book in connection with Reba McEntire's career, and who is one of the premier figures in the history of the Nashville music business.

"I am just as proud of the Suzy Bogguss signing as I am of the Garth Brooks signing or the George Strait signing or any of the others," he says. "Suzy had that magical something the first time I heard a tape that she made . . . I liked it very much; there was a wonderful warmth about it, and of course she has such a beautiful voice. And on the strength of that I agreed to go up to Dollywood to see her perform. I took our A & R director Terry Choate with me. She was performing—it was kind of a gazebo-type little stage . . . just she and her guitar, and she had some of her cassettes there [to sell to her fans]. There were benches there that—maybe you could have gotten fifty or sixty people in there if it were raining and crowded under the shelter, but at this time there were probably only about twenty of us. . . .

"I saw her perform and saw that wonderful personality and the eye contact she made with the people in the audience. A little bit later she took part in the bigger show on the main stage there; she did a couple of numbers.

"Driving back, her manager was riding with us and I said, 'Yeah, let's sign her, let's make a deal.'

"I was very unhappy with the first product we put out on her because it was not acoustic. I heard her . . . in the folk-acoustic country bag, you know, whatever you call that type of music, but definitely with a more acoustic feel. They were cutting some good songs and all but bigger productions than I felt they should have been, immediately putting her in competition with Reba as opposed to this little niche of being maybe the new Emmylou Harris. . . .

"Suzy is . . . extremely ambitious, very bright, she's beautiful and has the talent—you have to have the talent

Suzy Bogguss

. . . she always wanted this but she took her time before she wanted anybody to pitch her to a major label. She did coffeehouses and things of that type for about ten years before she really got her record deal.

"She had a manager, a radio person from up around Peoria . . . and she also had some backers. I have no idea what kind of investments people made. . . ."

Backers were people who believed in her and who were willing to invest money in her career. In most cases such money goes toward demo costs, publicity, etc. Usually the backers hope to make a profit on the deal. Occasionally the backers will do it strictly out of love for the artist and will be thrilled to recoup their expenses when the artist is successful, if they retain the friendship and the loyalty of the artist.

"Julie Henry, a local publicist, was the one who called me," Foglesong continued. "RCA did a fairly expensive studio audition demo tape of [Suzy]. It was recorded digitally in fact. Blake Mevis produced it for RCA and they turned her down. But Julie called me and she said, 'I just don't think they have the right feel but I think you and Suzy would get along great, I think you're the type person that would really work well with her and, anyway, I would just love for you to meet these people and hear the tape.'

"Well the audition tape, the RCA tape, wasn't nearly as impressive to me as the tape that she did with her friend in the studio, probably on a very limited budget. And to be honest with you, I didn't feel that the first product she cut for us was as good. We redid a couple of the same songs and they didn't come off as well as [the first little demo he heard].

"Some changes had to be made with Suzy. We experimented with a couple of producers before the right thing came along.

"I'm so pleased because I know how hard she's worked, how dedicated she is, and I know how hard she'll continue to work. It's so neat because sometimes, you know, you

Suzy with Chet Atkins.

sign people and the talent is there but the other little ingredients aren't there.''

How dedicated is she? Here's how David Zimmerman of *USA TODAY* described one phase of her career. ''[Her musical style] started drawing attention a dozen years ago when she graduated in metal smithing from Illinois University in Normal and developed 'little pockets' of listeners in Rocky Mountain resort areas.

''Often she did her own promoting, booking, and poster-plastering, building a circuit through Colorado, Wyoming, and Montana, and later from Chicago to Minneapolis.''

In her February 1993 article for *KNIX Country Spirit*, Sandy Lovejoy added that for many years Suzy was her own manager, did her own booking, and made her own travel arrangements. ''She is good at taking charge, and clever," Lovejoy added. "She created a secretary, Rachel ['Of course, it was just me with a dumb accent,' Suzy told Sandy], to make hotel reservations and other travel arrangements. That created the impression that she was a pro, not somebody you'd ask to perform at a backyard barbecue for a greasy rib."

She was so accustomed to doing it all herself that she was very cautious about hiring outside management, but eventually her career started getting so hectic that she had to give in.

"I talked to somebody from the label the other day," Foglesong continued, "and every country just about in the world now wants Suzy Bogguss to come over and do the interviews and do all the things they need to do to break her around the world." What he means is that employees of her label in many nations believe so much in Suzy that they think she could be a tremendous success in their country.

Her first records on Capitol came out in 1987 and within a year's time she had won the Academy of Country Music's Best New Country Female Vocalist Award.

"How many people have we seen that have had a couple of little bites, got something on the radio, or somehow they've been in the public eye, and then they've faded into obscurity?" Suzy said to Thomas Goldsmith, who was then a staff writer for the *Tennessean* and is now one of the most erudite freelance reporters on the Nashville scene.

"I thought if I'm going to fade into obscurity, I'm going to have a record I can play for people when I'm forty-five years old and say, 'I made this record; this is what I do.' "

There are a number of country artists today who take a view totally unlike that of the traditional country singer. Examples of such performers might be Mary Chapin Carpenter, Hal Ketchum, Kathy Mattea, and Suzy Bogguss, but there are a number of others. These people take their art seriously and want their music to be more than just commercially successful. They want it to be good. They want

Suzy receives the Horizon award in 1992.

to be proud of their work. Country music is better because of them.

"To me," she told Goldsmith, "this is a[n] . . . exciting time to be in this particular branch of music because

Suzy and Lee Greenwood "sing in the rain" at FanFair.

the integrity level has soared in the last three or four years. . . .

"There's less gimmicks and a lot more talent out there. . . . It's not a copy thing at all—that's the thing I'm finding most enticing.

"Everybody seems to be making their records now and it seems to be OK that this doesn't sound identical to somebody else. . . .

"What it's really done is spread itself out to where it's an interesting format. . . . That's the bottom line for me—it's far less trite than most of the other formats."

In 1991 Suzy surely must have been proud of her album "Aces," from which came three hits and a Horizon Award from the Country Music Association. This album was a breakthrough in that the tremendous airplay of its singles established her identity in the minds of many country listeners.

Her follow-up album, "Voices in the Wind," has continued to spread the word. It's a very satisfying album to listen to. The songs are well chosen, with strong lyrics, melodies that grab at you, and tremendous variety. She's not afraid to tackle a song that goes outside of standard country love themes, such as "Letting Go," a song written by Matt Rollings and her husband, Doug Crider, about a mother and her daughter who is about to leave for college; she does well with a pair of dramatic rhythm pieces written by John Hiatt, "Drive South" and "Lovin' a Hurricane"; and she eats up love songs like "Heartache," written by Lowell George and Ivan Ulz, and Richard Leigh's "Cold Day in July."

Jim Foglesong regards signing her as one of his proudest achievements. Jimmy Bowen will probably put out product on Suzy till the cows come home because she's that good. And she will win more awards. But will she ever be a platinum-selling artist? Yes.

15
Kathy Mattea

O F THE NEW CROP OF FOLKY COUNTRY ARTISTS, THE one with the veteran's credentials is Kathy Mattea. Over the past half dozen years she has built a great career on quality songs, songs like "Street Talk," "Love at the Five and Dime," "Eighteen Wheels and a Dozen Roses" and "Where Have You Been."

In the course of her long succession of unique hits her albums progressed to where they were selling gold. And then there were the awards: ACM Single of the Year, 1988; CMA Single of the Year, 1988; CMA Female Vocalist of the Year, 1989; ACM Top Female Vocalist, 1989; Radio and Records Country Readers Poll, Best Female Vocalist, 1990; and CMA Female Vocalist of the Year, 1990. She topped off the list in 1991 with a Grammy for Best (female) Country Vocal Performance.

Kathy was born in 1959 in South Charleston, West Virginia, and received her higher education at the University of West Virginia. A friend who played in the same bluegrass band as she did decided that he was going to move to Nashville and said that if she wanted to come along she could.

As she told the story to Vernell Hackett, "I said, 'Oh no, I can't come . . .' but the closer it came for him to come down I knew that I couldn't bear for him to be in Nashville in the music business and me not.

"This was 1978, September. So I got a job as a tour guide at the Country Music Hall of Fame and he was working as a waiter at Friday's and we took our tapes around and stuff and we met some people and the people would ask about my singing. . . .

"But after being around for awhile I knew enough to know that I would have to be a lot better, so I spent a few months being real intimidated."

After a few months her friend decided that he wasn't good enough to make it. But not Kathy. "I stayed and I knew I couldn't go back because I felt like I hadn't given it a fair shot. I knew that if I stayed, I really had to buckle down, so I got a voice teacher and started taking lessons. I got a job at an insurance agency so that I could pay for my voice lessons. Working as a tour guide was really getting to me.

"I did it [the insurance agency job] for about a year. I would go to work and I would come home and practice in my room for an hour and on Tuesday night I would go to Mississippi Whiskers and sit with the writers and all."

Mississippi Whiskers was a funky little club on Church Street that was one of Nashville's earliest listening rooms, where on Writers Night songwriters would gather to listen to each other's songs. It was a great opportunity for struggling songwriters to mix with established writers and listen to what they were doing that was not getting recorded.

"I was getting good enough to make a demo tape, so I went in the studio and did that and started taking it around and one guy started using me on some jingles and I started getting work here and there. . . ."

Nashville's premier music journalist Robert Oermann took her into Combine Music one day. Combine was one of the great independent music publishers that built the Nashville music industry before the world appeared on Nashville's doorstep in the eighties and bought up nearly every single one of them. Built by Fred Foster and Bob

Kathy Mattea receives her first CMA Award for "18 Wheels and a Dozen Roses" as Single of the Year.

Beckham, who are industry legends, the company was instrumental in the careers of people like Dolly Parton, Kris Kristofferson, and Larry Gatlin.

So Oermann brought Kathy into the Combine offices and began to rave about her singing. Publishing companies go through phases during which they will use one or another singer on most of their demos, which is good money for the lucky singer, and it just so happened that their usual female demo singer had moved to Los Angeles and they needed a new one.

It was the first time Kathy actually felt that she really might make her way on Music Row. "I wasn't sure that I would be able to find my place [in the music business] . . . where I fit in. I was afraid it would be so sewed up and everybody in the business would know each other so well and [I] was worried about how you get to know people or how you get into the group. That was my biggest fear."

Kathy's biggest fear then is the biggest fear of most newcomers. On the outside looking in, it always seems like there's a big glass wall between you and the music business. You can look through the wall and see what's going on, but you have to find a way to climb over it if you're going to be able to actually interact with the folks on the other side who seem so comfortable with each other. And that wall seems too hard to climb yourself. Usually it takes a bit of good fortune—which is what Kathy had when she and Oermann walked into Combine on the right day.

But after that first stroke of good luck, the talent and drive must be there, because there are plenty of people stumbling around *inside* that wall without a real career.

As often happens, after Combine started using Kathy on demos the word began to spread on Music Row and other publishers began to use her, including ATV Music. ATV was a West Coast-based company that owned many of Lennon's and McCartney's early copyrights, the ones that wound up in the hands of Michael Jackson. Working at ATV was a songwriter named Byron Hill. Byron saw to it that a tape of Kathy's demos went to Frank Jones, a music business veteran who had just been made head of Mercury Records in Nashville.

The result was her record deal with Mercury. Again Kathy was in luck. Sometimes a record company signs an artist and then spends months or years trying to figure out what to do with her. But Mercury was struggling and wanted a record out fast. Kathy signed her recording contract on her birthday, June 21, and on September 2, less than three months later, "Street Talk" hit the streets and immediately clicked on America's country radio stations. It

Kathy at Viewers Choice Award show.

Kathy at FanFair in 1991.

wasn't what the industry calls a monster, but it got into the twenties on the national charts and started Kathy on her way.

Kathy struggled for quite a number of years before she was in the right place at the right time, but once she got there her talent and common sense carried her a long way. For years she was produced by Alan Reynolds, one of Nashville's great music figures, a man responsible for so much of the success of Crystal Gayle, Garth Brooks, and Hal Ketchum. Alan falls in love with a great song when he hears it, and so does Kathy, and they made a potent combination when it came to putting out truly unique records. In recent times her album sales have dipped a bit and so Alan and Kathy have agreed to part professional company. Reynolds once told me that a producer and an artist shouldn't stay together more than a few years, I think he said three. After that time, he said, the creativity can begin to lag as the team attempts to reprise previous hit sounds.

So Kathy switched over to Brent Maher, the man who

produced all of the Judds' major successes, who like Reynolds has a reputation for cherishing great songs.

Success puts a tremendous amount of strain on an artist. Her time is not hers, nor is her privacy, nor is her voice. It was the voice that gave out on Kathy. For two years following her first CMA Vocalist of the Year Award she toured constantly and, most damaging, gave hundreds of interviews in between performances. Singers will tell you that talking, with its undisciplined strains upon the vocal chords, is generally more harmful than singing. This is especially so when the interviews are done backstage at concerts or in other places where the interviewee must shout over the background noise to be heard.

By 1992 Kathy's vocal cords were in bad shape and when she recorded her eighth album, "Lonesome Standard Time," she was aware she might have to undergo laser surgery on her vocal cords. "I sang with the knowledge of the possibility that I might not ever sing again," she said in a record company bio release. "Thank God I can. I savored every moment."

Fortunately, as in the case of Patty Loveless, her surgery was successful, but unlike Patty, the success of her album has been spotty. When an album does not live up to expectations, people try to figure out why radio and the folks didn't like it as well as previous offerings, but such inquiry is usually fruitless (The songs weren't as good? The singing wasn't as persuasive? The promotion department was concentrating on Billy Ray? The marketing department fell down on the job? The dance craze is putting folkies out of business?).

One CD is just one CD, and Kathy Mattea is still one of the most loved country artists in the business, with tremendously loyal fans.

Kathy knows there are many would-be artists who long to make it in the music business. She had these words for them, spoken into the tape recorder of Vernell Hackett. "I would say come prepared to stick it out for at least five years," she said, "before you evaluate where you are. Then decide whether you're going to stay or not. Always have the attitude that you want to keep learning . . . as long as you keep growing you'll have more and more to offer to people. Make sure that it is absolutely what you want to do. Really believe that this is where you belong. Because there's enough people that really believe that and they will endure longer than you if you don't.''

There's a tremendous amount of wisdom in that short paragraph. During her years in Nashville when she was working so hard to make progress she must have seen a few who made it, and so many more who fought the good fight for years and had very little to show for it. Obviously Kathy has not forgotten the years when she had to wonder whether or not it was ever really going to happen for her.

In 1988 Kathy married a tall young songwriter from Minnesota named Jon Vezner. Vezner is one of Nashville's premier songwriters. Besides having cowritten Kathy's best known hit, the multi-award-winning ''Where Have You Been,'' Jon's songs have been recorded by a number of country music's top artists, including Lorrie Morgan, Reba McEntire, Nanci Griffith, Faith Hill, and Steve Wariner.

As a successful songwriter, Jon has his own small measure of fame among fans who keep track of who writes the hits, and sometimes he will perform in various places around the country that schedule songwriter shows. But his face is not a famous face so he has privacy when he wishes. Kathy, on the other hand, does not have that choice. Jon has a unique opportunity to observe a celebrity every day and see how she responds to living in a fishbowl.

''When you opt for this sort of lifestyle particularly as an artist, and then you have a lot of trouble with people invading your privacy . . . you asked for it, it's part of it, you've got to accept it to a certain degree.

''There are situations where I've witnessed lots of artists, where fans will go, 'Here, sign this! Now sign this!' No 'thank you,' no anything like that. You become their property and I don't think that's correct. You are in the public eye but you're not necessarily their property.''

Kathy, posing for fans, has no idea that Shane Barmby is about to rope her.

Does an artist have the right to eat in a restaurant without somebody interrupting her mid-forkful?

"That's a hard call," Vezner said. "You would like to have that right but . . . again, if you're in the public eye it's going to happen. Face it, we all do this because we all clamor for some sort of attention on certain levels—artists on one level and songwriters at another level. I get as much of it as I want and then I can back out of it at any time. And artists can't do that."

Is Kathy philosophical all the time about the demands of public attention or does she have her moments when it's just too much?

"Well she has her moments. I think that part of when her voice went out was just being exhausted [from dealing so intensively with the public]. The singing is not the problem. It's the conversation. You have to be quiet. I mean she went through a period, it was real difficult but she had to not see her fans after the show . . . when she was going through this voice rest. She basically sang the shows and what they did was they brought back all the autograph [requests] and she signed them all in the [privacy] of her bus and then she maybe went out [to meet with her fans] for a couple of minutes.

"That's part of it that the people don't understand. Talking is the worst thing for your voice, particularly if you're tired and you talk too low . . . but there's another interesting thing too . . . you'll see certain artists where they'll go out and they'll be wearing sunglasses and all the stuff to 'be incognito' but they're anything but incognito. The way to be incognito is to go out in a sweatshirt and a T-shirt and no makeup. She does that all the time.

"Nashville's people are generally very cool and very respectful. They're very sweet and the up side of that is you get to meet a lot of very wonderful people. By and large the country fans are great.

"Where it's really interesting is where people come up and talk to you about what certain songs meant to them and their wife. And they feel like they need to tell you that."

Fans can't help but wonder how the image of their favorite star relates to the real nature of that person. Jon Vezner has this viewpoint for Kathy Mattea fans.

"Kathy is without a doubt . . . one of the most consistent people. What you see on stage, what you see is what you get, the same as I get at home I mean she is like that. She's real upbeat. She's very Italian and speaks her mind and she'll let you know what she thinks, which took some gettin' used to for me because I come from this northern European [background]—sort of stoic, you know. [Italians are] very expressive. They're quick to express their anger, they're quick to express their joy.

"I get this on the road all the time, promoters and stuff you know, one guy said, 'We get these artists and they get

Kathy at an early FanFair appearance.

up here and they're just jerks. They treat us badly, they have [absurd] demands, and Kathy rides in an RV with her in-laws and is exactly what you think she's gonna be.' ''

I think this promoter was saying that artists and their labels spend a lot of time and money promoting a positive image but that some of them, under the strain of touring and the exaggerated sense of self-importance that comes with image-building and fan adulation and believing their own press, do not come close to the image they cultivate. Kathy is a notable exception.

Kathy has a new producer, Josh Leo, whose approach to a recording is different from Brent Maher or Alan Reynolds. The industry is changing and Kathy's career is bound to change too. But, Jon points out, there are limits to the changes an artist will accommodate, if that artist has a sense of who she is and what she does.

"The way I see it is how far do you want to go to have a hit? You've gotta look at why you got into this in the first place. Radio's changing. It's real dance-driven and all that and I don't say that's bad but . . . she just can't try to change just to follow the market. You've got to listen to your own voice and that's what made it work for her in the first place and hopefully it'll come around—you know, it changes back and forth.

"I think there will always be a place for what we do, somewhere," he said, "the what we do" meaning the songs he writes, and the songs she sings, which are basically the same kind of songs.

As we go to press Kathy is working on a new album, in the never-ending quest for the next hit.

Kathy Mattea has been to the top and stayed for a number of years. She's still got the talent, the song sense, and the wonderful attitude that an artist owes it to her fans to give them her very best. As successful as she has been in the past, her biggest years may be in her future. *Billboard* columnist Ed Morris had this to say about Kathy:

"I still think she will get bigger and bigger. She's won the Country Music Association [Female] Vocalist of the Year Award twice without ever giving in to the market forces as far as I can tell.

"She shows her whimsical side. She has a great live show when she's doing her own commentary, and a voice that just won't quit, so I think Kathy will continue to sell

Kathy and Grand Ole Opry piano legend Del Wood.

records and win awards. I don't think Kathy Mattea's peaked yet. I think if she can get another 'Where Have You Been,' I think she will just go platinum. . . . She certainly has the talent for it.''

16

Pam Tillis

LIKE LORRIE MORGAN, PAM TILLIS GREW OUT OF A PRO-fessional music tradition. Her dad was the famous stuttering songwriter who slowly worked his way to international stardom.

To an outsider, having a famous father seems like a tremendous advantage for someone trying to get into the business. There is no doubt that there are some advantages, especially that of familiarity with the business. But it never looks quite as thrilling and simple from the inside as it does from the outside, as Pam recounted to interviewer Vernell Hackett.

"From the time I was three years old—my earliest memories were of wanting to be a singer, and all us kids used to perform in the living room, and Dad would get us all to show off for our relatives and that was my real start in show business."

When you're the daughter of a great singer-songwriter like Mel Tillis, you get to meet a lot of people in the business early. That tempers your awe of the business, which is a good thing. In an interview she did with Harlan Howard for an Arista promo CD, she recollected her childhood:

"When I think of who I was surrounded with and who

Pam Tillis

I thought of as my uncles,'' she said. ''Because we came up here from Florida, and so the rest of the family was still down there. You guys were our family to Daddy . . . and who did I have for uncles? Wayne Walker, Harlan Howard, Bobby Bare, Porter Wagoner, Kristofferson . . . boy, when I look back now, it's kind of overwhelming.

''What's interesting is, what I went through my own musical development and, I think I took it for granted . . . and then, when I started going back and listenin' to songs from that era, how could I not be moved? That's like openin' up family albums, you know. That's a slice of my life.''

But hanging around the big names when you're a child does not necessarily make you ready for the business when you grow up.

"It took me a long time to get my confidence together. I think certainly my dad being such a big star had something to do with that, it was a little intimidating. It wasn't apron strings I had to cut, I don't know, guitar strings? Whatever you want to call it."

"I was a basic misfit, and a professional partier," she told *Billboard*'s Timothy White. "And I think my temperament used to be much darker. I have a homemade ego—I didn't have much self-esteem or a strong emotional center, and constantly looked outside myself for it. I think some of it was genetic. The song 'Melancholy Child' on my first Arista album ["Put Yourself in My Place," 1991] was drawn from early childhood memories of my mom, who at sixteen or seventeen was a baby with a baby."

There was another reason for her self-doubts.

"I've always felt uncertain about my own attractiveness, thinking my appearance was kinda flawed," she told White. "But then, at sixteen I was in a car crash in which my face was shattered in over thirty places, from my cheeks down to my chin.

"My nose was flattened, my eye sockets were damaged, and it took five years of operations to put it all back together again. On days when the weather's odd, I still have pain, and the ongoing surgical upkeep makes me self-conscious sometimes about the angles of my album-cover photos or my video shoots."

Her dad had achieved success as a songwriter long before he hit his peak as an artist, with huge hits like "Detroit City" and "Ruby, Don't Take Your Love to Town," so Pam grew up with a superior understanding of the importance of songs in the career of an artist.

Consequently, she has compiled an impressive list of songwriter credits, with her songs recorded by stars like the late Conway Twitty, Highway 101, Ricky Van Shelton, Juice Newton, and Chaka Khan, as well as a number of

Pam at FanFair.

songs she has cowritten for herself in the course of her burgeoning recording career, including her recent smash, "Cleopatra, Queen of Denial."

Is she a singer, primarily, or a songwriter?

"To me it's always been a package," she told Vernell Hackett. "I never thought of myself as a performer, solely, or a songwriter. One thing kind of feeds off the other."

Before she was a recording artist she was a staff songwriter for Tree International, a publishing company whose name seems to pop up again and again whenever the subject of country music appears in print. That's because Tree is the most successful publishing company in the history of Nashville music. Its huge catalog includes most of the biggest hit songs of Willie Nelson, Roger Miller, Harlan Howard, Curley Putman, Hank Cochran, Red Lane, Bobby

Pam and husband Bob DiPiero.

Braddock, Sonny Throckmorton, Conway Twitty, Merle Haggard, and many others.

You'll notice that all these songwriters are men. For most of its history Tree had few women writers on staff. But Nashville has changed and so has Tree. While most of its writers are still men, there are a number of prominent women there now, and the head of the company, which is owned by Sony, is Donna Hilley.

Warner Brothers Records signed Tillis and many of the people there really expected her to happen, but she didn't. Not there. Why not? Why ask. She just didn't.

Arista Records was a different story, however. Arista is a special story because Tim DuBois, who is the Nashville head of Arista, is a special person. A songwriter turned producer turned record executive, Tim was hired to head the brand new country division of Clive Davis's prosperous record company. In no time at all he had signed, and established Alan Jackson, Diamond Rio, Brooks and Dunn, and Pam Tillis, with Michelle Wright ever so close.

Once Pam had signed with Arista it was not long before hits like "Don't Tell Me What to Do" and "Maybe It Was Memphis," were telling radio and the fans that a big new star had arrived.

She told Harlan how she came to cut "Don't Tell Me What to Do," which was written by Harlan and Max D. Barnes. "Marty Stuart—I used to go see him play before he had a lot happenin'—and I don't know if he recorded that, but he used to sing that song and I thought, 'Boy, that'd be a great girl's song,' and I just loved the song and I sat on that thing for I guess about five years.

"We [Pam and her producer, Paul Worley] were going through songs for the album, just down to the wire, and we needed one more thing, one more hit on that package.

"And I promise you . . . the last tape [we were going to listen to] I said, 'Paul, I don't know why I hadn't thought of this, this is one of my favorite songs, I've been draggin' this tape around, listen to this!'

"Course, one of the reasons I hadn't played it for him is we'd cut most of my own things. He listened to it and just about fell out of his chair and he went, 'Tillis, where's this tape been? . . . We're cuttin' that tomorrow.' " The next day they cut a hit record.

Her album, "Homeward Looking Angel," is well past gold in sales, with a trio of classic radio hits, "Let That

Pony Run,'' ''Shake the Sugar Tree,'' and ''Cleopatra, Queen of Denial'' providing the everyday exposure that has driven the sales of the album. The album is a fine mixture of songs Pam cowrote and songs she didn't, and the overall quality of songs is so impressive that you know she's learned the most important of all Music Row lessons: It all begins with a song.

Only now is Pam Tillis really finding her footing as a recording artist, and if ''Homeward Looking Angel'' is a measure of the future, she will be a powerful force in country music for years to come.

17
Wynonna Judd

THERE IS ONE FEMALE COUNTRY SINGER WHOSE DEBUT album has gone triple platinum. It's not Reba. It's not Dolly. It's not Trisha. It's Wynonna.

Back in April of 1992 a West Coast critic reviewed Wynonna's first solo album for one of America's premier papers. He gave the album a two-and-a-half-star rating, which is halfway between "good" and "fair."

In the review he wrote, "What is surprising is that a singer with one of the most potent, versatile voices in country music—in any area of pop, for that matter—seems so timid about putting a lot of feeling into [the songs]." After complimenting her on her varied range of styles, then complaining about the uneven nature of the material, he concluded by stating that "In this first flight out of the nest, Judd seems intimidated by her potential power, and she restrains her expressiveness as if she's afraid to let it soar. That's what everybody has been waiting for, and it looks as if they'll have to wait a little longer."

The album he was talking about was "Wynonna," the one that has sold more than three million. The critic had given a mediocre review to what would be one of the most successful albums in the history of female country singers. What gives here? Has this guy got a tin ear or was he having a bad day?

Probably neither. He was simply giving us his honest

Wynonna Judd in concert in 1988.

opinion, and it is fairly obvious that he'd listened to the album with great care, wanted to hear a great album, and did not. That his opinion did not gibe with the opinions of millions of Americans is not necessarily a reflection of his taste. After all, nowhere in his review did he say, ''I do not think the folks will like this album.'' All he said, basically, was, I think this is a fair to good album. His honest opinion, take it or leave it.

Nobody knows. Most fans somewhere along the line will jump on what they thought was a crowded bandwagon only to find that even as they were jumping on, everybody else was getting off. Every record producer has at one time or another recorded what he thought was the next Elvis or Hank Williams, Sr., only to find that the fans don't agree, and if the fans don't agree, there's nothing more to say. Every head of A & R, no matter how timid, sooner or later has to make a decision to sign an act, and most of the time the executive guesses wrong, because a lot more acts flop than succeed.

Many other reviewers, however, thought highly of that first solo album. *Rolling Stone*, for example, gave it four stars out of a possible five and called it "an album informed by integrity and wisdom, begging no classification save that of powerful, stirring, ennobling music."

Back in the late seventies a middle-aged man and his young, blond daughter, who had been knocking around the country scene for a decade, suddenly burst into prominence with a song called "Heaven's Just a Sin Away." They followed this monster hit with several other songs in a similar vein. Now, what was the image there, of this father and daughter act singing almost gospel-sounding songs about cheatin' and sinnin'? The image may have been a bit murky, but the records were great, and the folks were buying records, not image.

Now the year is 1984, George Orwell's fateful year of reckoning. There is a new act out, a mother-daughter act, and lookie here, the mother is so cute she could break the heart of any young man anywhere, while her young daughter is still in her awkward years. But like the father-daughter duo, the Kendalls, the Judds are primarily a showcase for the daughter, with the parent providing the tight harmonies that make for unique sounding records, and who cares what the image is supposed to be?

Woody Bowles, who co-managed them during the formative stages of their career, talked about how the Judds hit the stardom that they both, in their own ways, dreamed of. "In June of '82 I met Naomi at the Music City News Awards—I was doing publicity for Ricky Skaggs and she'd just kinda been standing backstage. I don't know what, for sure, she was doing other than trying to meet people. I found out later that they'd been in town for about five years and had been knocking on doors and doing Ralph Emery's morning show and all, but anyway, she came up to me and introduced herself and told me that she and her daughter sang, you know, one of the same old stories that we hear a million times.

"I wasn't short with her but I was focused [on other things, like his job]. 'Well, it's nice to meet you,' she asked for one of my cards, I gave her a card and kind of politely brushed her aside and went on doing what I was doing with Ricky. It was so strange, I was at an NEA [Nashville Entertainment Association] meeting one afternoon—this was a couple of weeks later—and I came back to my office . . . and I walked into the building about four in the afternoon and the smell of this incredible strong lilac perfume came wafting down the stairway. I'm real sensitive to that, started getting a headache immediately.

"I came into the office and Wynonna and Naomi were sitting there in the outer office. I went on into my office and the secretary came in. I said, 'What are they doing here?' and she said, 'Well they're here for their four o'clock appointment.' And I said, 'Well, I haven't made a four o'clock appointment with them.' She said, 'I didn't think you had either but they swear they've got a four o'clock appointment with you.'

"I went ahead and saw them. I figured, hey if they're this brash let's see what the deal is. They came in and sat and talked and Naomi told me all kinds of stuff about how she had written a semiautobiographical story of the lives of this mother and daughter who come to Nashville and make it big on the Grand Ole Opry, and she had this idea of a radio show she wanted to do, just all this stuff, you know, but it was all stuff Naomi was doing and she had her modeling portfolio with her—I wasn't exactly sure why the daughter was along. I listened to this rambling for about an hour and I said, listen, you guys, you want to let me hear you sing?

"Wynonna had brought her guitar so they broke out the guitar and started singing songs and Wynonna literally nailed me to the wall with her voice. That first day they sang 'Mama He's Crazy,' they sang 'Change of Heart,' they sang that song that was on the first mini-LP, 'I'm Like a John Deere Tractor in a Half-Acre Field'—these were three of the six songs that [would be] on that first mini-LP.

"I saw the potential there. They told me that they had chosen Brent Maher to be their producer and I had known Brent for years so I just called Brent up one day and I said, 'Do you know this Naomi and Wynonna Judd?' and he said, 'Yeah, as a matter of fact the mother was my daughter's nurse (when his daughter had had an automobile wreck) while she was in the hospital.'

"I said, 'Have you heard them sing?' He said, 'Well they gave me a tape of some stuff they had done at home and it's really strange. I'm not sure what we have here.'

"I said, 'Well they've come in and sung for me and I'd like to get together with you if you're interested at all because I think I know what we could do with them.' So he and I kinda teamed up and started going out and sitting with them at their house and listening to all this repertoire of old stuff. They were into some old Andrews Sisters and even before them, Hazel and Alice, I think they were called. We combed through records and there was a lot of Bonnie Raitt influence in Wynonna of course.

"I had known Ken Stilts because he had hired me to do a PR program on Eddie Raven, and I knew that we were gonna need money. Ken had another company, a gasket and fiberglass company in Mount Juliet [a small city east of Nashville] and he'd dabbled in putting together a little label called Dimension Records—I think they'd had a Ray Price hit—I knew that to pull this thing off we were gonna need money because for me to go to work on a project like that at that time I needed to be paid while I was working on it. The girls themselves had no money, Naomi was emp-

Mother Naomi and Wynonna at the CMA Awards.

tying bedpans all night long and was trying to pursue music with Wynonna during the day. They had been turned down by every record label in town, just about.

"Ken came to see the girls at my office one afternoon and he really liked what he saw. It was a matter of if we could get something going he'd be interested [in backing the deal].

"On the fourth of January, 1983, I was in Los Angeles with Elaine [his brand new wife] for a movie junket on *Ghandi*—they'd flown us out there since she was doing *Entertainment Tonight*. While we were out there I went to see my old buddy Dick Whitehouse."

Dick Whitehouse had worked for Mike Curb's record and production companies for years. He is based in California and is highly regarded by Nashville producers and talent managers, who seek him out for record and production deals.

"I had been doing some work for him on the Burrito

Brothers. We were sitting and talking and [I told him] 'Dick, I've got this group that you've got to see, this mother and daughter and the mother's real pretty and the daughter's a little heavy but she just sings great and they do some harmonies together and it's just unbelievable. They've got some great songs and you've just gotta come to Nashville and see these two.'

"It was like, 'Woody, I don't even drive down to the Palomino to see anybody anymore. Give me a tape.'

"I said, 'Listen, we don't have a tape, we don't have a picture, nothing on them. Now, you've gotta hear them sit down and do this thing.'

"He said, 'Look, go back to Nashville. I'll give you a hundred dollars. Take them in [the studio]. Just do a guitar vocal on them.' I got back in town that weekend and called Brent and told him what Dick had said. So we went over to Creative [Brent's studio] that Monday night and took them in and did just a guitar vocal thing on three songs where Wynonna played the guitar, but then we did the three-part harmonies and did the vocals really right.

"I turned around on Tuesday and FedExed [the tape] to Dick Whitehouse and on Wednesday afternoon I got a call back from Whitehouse and the message he had left was 'On a scale of one to ten this is an eleven! I'm coming to Nashville.'

"Whitehouse came on in [to Nashville and told us] 'I'm real interested in this, what do you all want?'

"And I said, well, 'I'd like to see you do an RCA affiliation.' At the time Curb's way of doing business was doing joint deals with various labels like MCA or Capitol. In recent years they have turned their efforts toward building the Curb Record label, which is at this time home to stars such as Sawyer Brown and Hal Ketchum.

"I had really looked at it. I was really impressed with what Galante (Joe Galante, then head of RCA in Nashville, now head of RCA, period) was doing over there. Whitehouse had his relationships at Warner Brothers also at that time but the Whites were over at Warner Brothers and I

Naomi and Wynonna test Randy Travis at a CMA Show.

felt that would be too much inter-label conflict. They [and the Judds] weren't exactly alike but they were somewhat similar stylistically to what we envisioned at the beginning [for the Judds]. Anyway he said, 'I don't have an RCA deal' and I said, 'Well look, you're a big man, you've got ninety days to get one. If you can pull together an RCA affiliation then we'll do a deal.'

"And Joe Galante and Randy Goodman in February were out in L. A. for the Grammy Awards. Whitehouse got them off in a motel room and played them this same tape over a Walkman. They loved it. It took us a month but we got a meeting set up for them to come in and sing for Galante. Whitehouse flew in for that; he got in just a few minutes late. In the room that day were me and Brent, Joe Galante, Randy Goodman, Tony Brown, and Norro Wilson (two staff A & R men) and Naomi and Wynonna. Interesting group of people. They came in, sang those songs, talked and did the spiel.

"Brent and I and the girls went down to O'Charley's [a restaurant near Music Row] and left Whitehouse there with

Galante and them. Within an hour Whitehouse joined us at O'Charley's and said, 'Congratulations, y'all are RCA/Curb artists.'

"That was in March of '83. In June of that year Wynonna showed up on our doorstep—this was the month they were to start recording their mini-LP—and Wynonna showed up at our door on Friday night and said, 'Momma's kicked me out of the house.'

"Brent had first made me aware that there were some difficulties between the girls. They were two hours late for their first meeting with Dick Whitehouse when he flew in because of a fight they were having. But I really believed in what was happening there and I guess in my naiveté I felt like I could fix them [laughs].

"She had no place to go so we said, 'Yeah, you can stay here with us for awhile.' She was there when our twins were born in November, in fact she lived with us for a year."

Woody later considered that taking her in caused problems because Naomi might have viewed him as taking sides with Wynonna in their continuing mother-daughter quarrels.

"The fights that would go on were very unsettling because of the level of the ferocity. I never knew from one day to the next whether this thing was gonna hold together or not. . . . But I was gonna be the savior that was gonna straighten them out." Here he laughed at his own naive conceit.

"The first single that came out was 'Had a Dream,' and it went to number seventeen on the *Billboard* chart. March of '84 was when 'Mama He's Crazy' was released."

That was the one that put the Judds on top. It had been written by Kenny O'Dell, especially for the Judds, three or four years earlier, according to Woody. The next album, "Why Not Me," went platinum.

One after another their great singles hit the radio. They came out like clockwork, along with albums that were perennial favorites. Total sales climbed to more than ten million, and they laid claim to seven Country Music Association awards. The Judds were one of those acts that the country industry dreams of—high-quality, hardworking, good for a decade or more of selling albums.

And then Naomi announced that she had contracted chronic hepatitis and would have to give up performing. You can imagine how it hit Wynonna. "I have dreams that mom dies and comes back and dies and comes back," she told *People* magazine. "I have it several times in a week."

Wynonna was born in 1964 in Ashland, Kentucky, but her name was Christina, and at the age of four the family moved to California, then, six years later, back to Kentucky. "That was when I discovered music," she recalled. "My influences—I thank God for this now—were the records from the old record shops, the used bins. Bluegrass was my first influence, and the mountain harmonies, the mountain soul of Hazel and Alice, the harmonies of the family from the Delmore Brothers, the Stanley Brothers and the Louvin Brothers. And then I started listening to Bonnie Raitt. She's been one of the biggest influences on my vocal style. I also remember being drawn toward old music. Instead of Top 40, I was listening to big band, and I was listening to the stuff that my grandparents danced to on the weekends. I was pretty eclectic."

I'd like to pick up on this a little. Most country stars enjoy feeling close to their fans. They enjoy knowing what their fans like, and, unlike a lot of pop stars, they respect their fans and try not to "get above their raisin'."

One of the biggest gaps between country artists and their fans is that while most country fans seem to be devoted to country music only, many country artists love all kinds of music. Even a traditionalist like George Strait loves Frank Sinatra. I've talked about how many of the female artists enjoy stretching their music far beyond their country roots. When you love certain kinds of music, you want to use them; rest assured that somewhere down the road Wynonna will want to record with a big band sound.

Anyway, Wynonna was one of those kids who got so

Naomi, Amy Grant, and Wynonna.

involved with music that that's about all she did in her spare time. When she was fifteen she and her family moved to Franklin, Tennessee, a city outside of Nashville that is in the midst of evolving from a rural community to an upscale suburb. Her mom encouraged her music, and Wynonna took a total plunge into it. "I became so involved with music," she said, "that I was way out in left field. I didn't go to dances, I didn't date. I didn't discover boys until I was eighteen or nineteen."

We've read how so many future stars started entertaining professionally in their tender years. But Wynonna was just sitting home alone, listening to records, singing and playing her guitar, and dreaming of being part of the real music world. Naomi (whose name was Diana) fretted like most mothers would and tried to get her daughter to go out and get a job. But in the meantime they were trying to get into the music business. And when they did, their lives changed suddenly, and forever.

And now Wynonna's first solo album is history, one of the most successful albums in the history of female country recording. Her second album, "Tell Me Why," is out, and platinum after only three months. The first two singles off the album have virtually chewed up the charts. With the publicity, praise, and success granted a number of the other women, it is Wynonna who might wind up being the most powerful of them all.

18

And Finally . . .

THIS BOOK HAS COVERED A NUMBER OF WOMEN, BUT not all of them. Missing are a number of artists of the future like Lucinda Williams, Lisa Stewart, Linda Davis, Stephanie Davis, and others.

Also missing are many artists of the past because the history chapter was just a brief background note. To anyone interested in the history of women in country music, I suggest Mary A. Bufwack and Robert K. Oermann's book, *Finding Her Voice: The Saga of Women in Country Music*, which I believe stands as a definitive history of women in country music.

There are also two women of the present that I have not yet talked about, but will now. They are K. T. Oslin and Roseanne Cash. They were hit artists in the eighties, and they will have more success in the nineties.

But they are artists who made a place for themselves in country music because only country music was broad enough to hold them.

That's right, I said *broad* enough. Many in the national press love to characterize country music as narrow and restrictive. In fact, as other popular music genres have become more and more restrictive, country music has become the logical home for a number of artists whose music is more song-dominated than production-dominated.

But country music was not meant to be a catchall for neglected styles. The urban cowboy slide followed by the new traditionalist boom should have proved to record executives that country fans, including lots of young country fans, will buy young artists singing real country music.

In another day and time, Roseanne and K. T. would have been perfect for the fans who listened to Carole King and Joni Mitchell records on the radio. But today it's hard to find places on the radio dial, or on TV, for words-and-music artists. Our aging baby boomers are going for mellower music than they did in their bad ol' counter-culture days. It would be great if some record mogul finally figured out a successful, hit-driven music format that would take the pressure off country music as a depository for song-driven pop acts.

Such a format would be a home for great ballads and solid rhythm records. Nobody would complain that it had too many string parts and not enough fiddles and steel. Nashville could cut all the music it would love to cut if the home offices would let it, and artists like K. T. Oslin, Roseanne Cash, and Linda Ronstadt would have a home for their great music over the next decade.

Of course, getting radio to see the merits of such a format would be difficult. Radio is like the record industry. Copy, copy, copy.

Not long ago I saw a new girl on CMT. New for me, that is. She's been around for awhile but only now are folks like myself beginning to discover her. Her name is Iris DeMent and she is so country she makes Patty Loveless sound like Barbra Streisand. She's so good but so different that she has a chance to hit the music world like a storm. She also has a chance to sail through like a cool breeze, changing little on the way but leaving a handful of devoted fans in her path. In the world of popular music, including country, it's hard to predict how fans will react. That's why record executives get fired so often.

Iris is the youngest of fourteen children, reared around

Paragould, Arkansas, and had gone to waitress in Kansas City, Missouri. Thank heavens for Rounder Records, a Boston folk label that believes somehow you can get by signing artists on their talent and uniqueness rather than their packageability. They put out an album on her called "Infamous Angel," which somebody at Warner Brothers discovered and loved. They acquired the album from Rounder and have released it. It's wonderful. Imagine an Emmylou Harris or a Dolly Parton who spent her formative years listening to Kitty Wells records and started writing songs.

"I remember being about four or five and making up songs," she said in a 1991 piece that was used as liner notes on her album. "I'd be outside playing and I'd make up a song about mom's flowers. I remember it hit me like, Wow! This is really neat! You can make up your own songs!"

She made up some excellent ones for her album.

Billy Altman's review for *Entertainment Weekly* summed her up neatly. "Listen to Iris DeMent for a few minutes," he wrote, "and you begin to understand why country and folk music have begun to rediscover each other for the first time since the Hootenanny days of the '60s. With an unaffected, snow-pure voice and a batch of honest, adult songs about love, home, and family so good you'd swear you've heard them before, she seems to be a single-bodied reincarnation of the entire Carter family. I hear America singing—and it sounds like Iris DeMent."

Whether or not she hits big the important thing is that Warner Brothers got interested and signed her. By the way, this album, with its spare, folky, very traditional country sound, was produced in Nashville, by producer Jim Rooney, Alan Reynolds's studio associate on a number of commercially successful projects.

The girls of country music might not sell like the boys do, not yet, but they have come a long way over the past decade. Most of the record labels in Nashville believe in them and keep signing new ones, good ones. By the time you read this book, some of those who have been trying for awhile will have made it, while others whom you have not heard of will appear out of nowhere. What a great time for the girls in country music.

The Best in Biographies from Avon Books

IT'S ALWAYS SOMETHING
by Gilda Radner   71072-2/ $5.95 US/ $6.95 Can

RUSH!
by Michael Arkush
                        77539-5/ $4.99 US/ $5.99 Can

STILL TALKING
by Joan Rivers   71992-4/ $5.99 US/ $6.99 Can

CARY GRANT: THE LONELY HEART
by Charles Higham and Roy Moseley
                        71099-9/ $5.99 US/ $6.99 Can

I, TINA
by Tina Turner and Kurt Loder
                        70097-2/ $5.50 US/ $6.50 Can

ONE MORE TIME
by Carol Burnett   70449-8/ $4.95 US/ $5.95 Can

PATTY HEARST: HER OWN STORY
by Patricia Campbell Hearst with Alvin Moscow
                        70651-2/ $5.99 US/ $6.99 Can

SPIKE LEE
by Alex Patterson   76994-8/ $4.99 US/ $5.99 Can